Brownstone Mystery Guides
ISSN 1055-6859
Volume Fourteen

Murder Most Poetic

THE MYSTERY NOVELS OF NGAIO MARSH

BY
MARY S. WEINKAUF

EDITED BY MARY A. BURGESS

BORGO PRESS / WILDSIDE PRESS

www.wildsidepress.com

Copyright © 1996 by Mary S. Weinkauf

Library of Congress Cataloging-in-Publication Data

Weinkauf, Mary S. (Mary Stanley), 1938-
    Murder most poetic : the mystery novels of Ngaio Marsh / by Mary S.
Weinkauf ; edited by Mary A. Burgess.
    p. cm. — (Brownstone mystery guides, ISSN 1055-6859 ; v. 14)
    Includes bibliographical references and index.
    ISBN 0-89370-197-1 (cloth). — ISBN 0-89370-297-8 (pbk.)
    1. Marsh, Ngaio, 1895-1982—Criticism and interpretation. I. Burgess,
Mary Wickizer, 1938- . II. Title. III. Series.
PR9639.3.M27Z94 1996   95-5336
823—dc20   CIP

FIRST EDITION

CONTENTS

ABOUT MARY S. WEINKAUF

MARY S. WEINKAUF received her doctorate in English, specializing in Milton and the British Renaissance, in 1966, and served as assistant professor of English at Adrian College until 1969, when she moved to Dakota Wesleyan University in Mitchell, South Dakota. She was Professor of English, Head of the English Department, and Chairman of the Humanities Division until 1989.

Dr. Weinkauf is the author of *Hard-Boiled Heretic: The Lew Archer Novels of Ross Macdonald* (Brownstone/Borgo, 1994) and *Sermons in Science Fiction: The Novels of S. Fowler Wright* (Borgo Press, 1994). She has also published articles on Milton, science fiction, utopian thought, and mystery fiction in *Studies in English Literature*, *Tennessee Studies in Literature*, *Extrapolation*, *Riverside Quarterly*, *Midwest Review*, *Clues*, and other scholarly periodicals, as well as reviews, poems, devotional writing, and short stories.

In 1989 she left college teaching to enroll in Lutheran School of Theology at Chicago, where she earned her Master of Theology degree in 1993. She now serves Siloa and Faith Lutheran Churches, Evangelical Lutheran Church in America, in Michigan's Upper Peninsula, works with Habitat for Humanity, Interfaith Volunteer Caregivers, hospice and sexual violence counseling.

In tribute to her family's affection for Ngaio Marsh, one of Weinkauf's grandchildren was named Roderick Alan.

A NGAIO MARSH CHRONOLOGY

1895 Edith Ngaio Marsh is born at Christchurch, New Zealand on April 23rd, the daughter of Henry Edmund Marsh, a bank clerk, and Elizabeth "Rose" Seager Marsh, an actress.

1910 (through 1914) Educated at St. Margaret's College, Christchurch.

1915 (through 1920) Attended Canterbury University College School of Art, Christchurch.

1920 (through 1923) Actress in New Zealand.

1923 (through 1927) Theatrical producer in New Zealand.

1928 (through 1932) Interior decorator in partnership with Mrs. Tahu Rhodes, London.

1933 (through 1943) Returned to New Zealand where she served in a New Zealand Red Cross transport unit during World War II.

1934 Her first crime novel, *A Man Lay Dead*, featuring Inspector/Superintendent Roderick Alleyn is published in London by Bles.

1938 Marsh's detective, Roderick Alleyn, meets and falls in love with a painter, Agatha Troy in *Artists in Crime*.

1941 Marsh begins a 30-year association with the Student Drama Society of Canterbury University College (her alma mater).

1944 (through 1952) Producer for D. D. O'Connor Theatre Management in New Zealand.

1948 Is made a Fellow in the Royal Society of Arts, and receives her O.B.E. (Officer, Order of the British Empire).

1951 (through 1952) Artistic director for the British Commonwealth Theatre Company.

1962 Receives her D. Litt. from Canterbury University.

1965 *Black Beech and Honeydew: An Autobiography* is published in Boston by Little, Brown.

1966 Receives her D.B.E. (Dame Commander, Order of the British Empire).

1967 Honorary Lecturer in Drama at Canterbury University

1977 Recipient of the Mystery Writers of America Grand Master award.

1982 Dame Ngaio Marsh dies on February 18. Her last novel, *Light Thickens*, is published in London by Collins and in Boston by Little, Brown.

I.

THE PLAY'S THE THING

NGAIO MARSH AS PRODUCER-DIRECTOR OF CLASSIC MYSTERIES

When *Light Thickens* was published posthumously in 1982, the novel, which can be described as probably the best portrait of a working theatrical company which its author has produced, was an appropriate concluding chapter to the life of a woman who had balanced a successful career as producer and director with another as the creator of thirty-two detective novels about a man named after an Elizabethan tragedian. Although she has been ranked with Dorothy Sayers, Agatha Christie, and Marjory Allingham as one of the great women writers of the classic British detective story, Ngaio Marsh won her recognition and title as Dame Commander of the Order of the British Empire (OBE) in 1966 for her career as a Shakespearean director-producer. In her autobiography, *Black Beech and Honeydew*, she playfully explained:

> If I have any indigenous publicity value it is, I think, for work in the theatre rather than for detective fiction....Intellectual New Zealand friends tactfully avoid all mention of my published work, and if they like me, do so, I cannot but feel, in spite of it.[1]

She goes on to express amazement that she is known outside her native New Zealand.

As one of New Zealand's most famous authors, Marsh wrote a small and loving book about her country for juvenile audiences, indicating her pride in her nation's beauty, education, government, interracial respect, and cultural life, but typically modest, she never mentioned her own novels, *Died in the Wool*, *Colour Scheme*, *Vintage Murder*, and *Photo Finish*, which are all set in New Zealand and which also portray its people, landscape, and lore.

She does, however, report proudly on the growth of the movement to emphasize drama in schools and universities, on the fact that school children design, build, and paint their own scenery, and that the University of Canterbury's student Drama Society operates in exactly the way a professional company does, by making profits. Drama Society members, she reports, have entered professional companies in England, toured New Zealand and Australia, and have won various state scholarships. One member toured America with the Old Vic Company. Appropriately, when the Drama Society used its profits to build a new theater at Canterbury University, it was named after Ngaio Marsh, in recognition of her contributions to its success.

Born in 1895, Marsh shared her birthdate, April 23rd, with her beloved Shakespeare (a date which also crops up in several of her novels). Her father, Henry Edmund Marsh, had attended Dulwich College, which was founded by Edward Alleyn, a renowned Elizabethan actor. One of Marsh's paternal ancestors, a Governor of the Tower of London, was said to have influenced Charles II to be merciful to George Fox, founder of the Quakers. She has often explained that Alleyn was given his name and affinity with the theater in honor of her father's school. Alleyn's confidant and working partner, Edward Fox, would seem to have been named in a similar manner, in tribute to her earlier ancestor.

Ngaio's mother, Elizabeth Seager Marsh—"Rose" as she was called—was such a gifted amateur actress that she eventually had offers to become a professional. Rose appeared in plays all throughout her daughter's childhood, thus setting the stage for young Ngaio to meet and know her mother's colleagues who made their livings in the theater. Rose made no protest when her daughter chose the theater as a profession.

Another significant influence was Dame Ngaio's maternal grandfather who was an early member of the (then) newly-founded New Zealand police force, and who helped design a uniform for it. She reports that he made at least two exciting arrests, one of "a famous sheep-stealer," and another "a gigantic Negro murderer."2 He presented her with a cherished theatrical relic, Kean's coat, which she later passed on to Sir Laurence Olivier after seeing him perform Richard III.3 Eventually her grandfather became the superintendent of a mental asylum where he directed plays as therapy for the patients. Marsh was blessed with loving, interesting relatives. An only child, she remained dedicated to her parents' well-being, and was devastated by her mother's death. She remained with her father, caring for him for the rest of his life.

Ngaio Marsh was also fortunate in her education. Her early training was in painting, an interest that is reflected in the way her detective protagonist views his world, and it is especially significant that Alleyn's wife is depicted as one of England's greatest artists. Writing obviously became one of her chief talents. Marsh attended St. Margaret's, a private school run by Anglo-Catholic sisters, where she was given what she calls a great gift by a dedicated English teacher—her love of Shakespeare. During her stay at St. Margaret's, Marsh wrote a version of *Cinderella* which was performed by her fellow students.

Her university training in art was supported through scholarships. Her first published article was a piece on travel for the *Sun*, for which she became a regular contributor. Certainly her painter's eye and affinity with people made her a delightful observer. When we see New Zealand through Troy's eyes in *Photo Finish*, Marsh is demonstrating her own skill of portrayal which characterized her early fiction pieces, as well as the two non-fiction books on New Zealand.

When the Allan Wilkie Shakespeare Company toured New Zealand, Marsh was enchanted by the acting she witnessed in *Hamlet*. She sent her play, *The Medal-*

lion, to Wilkie, and he and his wife, a leading actress of the time, encouraged her work. In 1920 they invited her to join their company for the winter tour. For the impressionable young woman, the theatrical tour was a kind of dream-come-true experience—one which she would later reprise when Martyne Tarne and Peregrine Jay experience it in *Night at the Vulcan* and *Killer Dolphin*, respectively.

Marsh's first professional acting stint was, prophetically enough, in a "Bulldog Drummond"-type thriller. She began to understand the energy and excitement which drew people to the stage, and the full experience of traveling with a professional troup is vividly recreated by Marsh in *Vintage Murder* (which is dedicated to her mentors the Wilkies). When Ngaio Marsh entered the world of the theater she recognized that she had joined another loving "family" which closely-paralleled her own supportive home life. Her delight with that tight-knit unity of actors, stage managers, dressers, and night watchmen is recreated faithfully throughout her works, which invariably deal with theatrical life and with the performers who live it.

Marsh toured several times, once with an amateur group including some of her own friends and her mother who performed her own play, *Little Housebound*. Another tour was with a company playing comedy. Although Marsh admits that she had some rather innocent "romances" with fellow actors and was once engaged, she never married. The theater remained her home, and the young budding actors and actresses of Canterbury University were her children.

While Marsh was in Christchurch she encountered the delightful family she called the Lampreys, the only "real" people upon whom she intentionally based any of her mysteries. The Lampreys were natural aristocrats with noble ties but who scarcely ever had the funds to support their expensive tastes and love of new experiences. The family is featured in *Death of a Peer* (*A Surfeit of Lampreys*); the boy Mike appears in *Killer Dolphin* as an amazingly literate young police constable who trades Shakespearean quotations with an arrogant playwright; and Julia Pharamond, who captivates Alleyn's son Ricky in *Last Ditch*, admits to being a Lamprey. The family opened their hearts to young Marsh, and she was dazzled by their flamboyant lifestyle. When they departed for England in hopes of improving their financial fortunes, Marsh visited them and finally became acquainted with the country she had heard about all her life.

From 1928 to 1932 Marsh lived in London and worked as an interior decorator and co-owner of a shop. She wrote travel articles and worked desultorily on a novel set in New Zealand (which remained unfinished). Never a great reader, Marsh did, however, fatefully select a detective novel from a Bourne Street lending library and read it through one rainy Sunday when her mother was away visiting with friends. She had given some thought to writing a crime novel, so the book with which she serendipitously filled her spare time provided her with further inspiration. A discussion on how she got started follows:

> The Murder Game was fashionable in those days. It was an elaborate house-party diversion played out in the dark. "Suppose" I had thought in a blaze of inspiration, "suppose instead of a pretence corpse, a real one was found." I imagine some round dozen of established practitioners had already discarded this *trouvaille* as being too obvious but I thought it was just fine. And now, on this wet Sunday, I went to the newspaper shop that was always open in Bourne Street and bought several penny exercise books and some sharpened pencils. I don't think that before or since this weekend I have ever written with less trouble and certainly never with less distinction.[4]

The penny notebooks turned into a pile. One day she came home from her shop to find her mother reading one of them, and Mrs. Marsh admitted that she couldn't put it down. By 1934 Bles had published *A Man Lay Dead* and had contracted for Marsh's next three novels. She never looked back.

By this time Marsh's mother had become seriously ill, and together they returned to New Zealand. She settled down to writing in earnest, and at the same time began her career as producer/director for the D. D. O'Connor Theatre—the British Commonwealth Theatre Company. She also pursued her studies in Shakespeare at Canterbury University (from which she received an honorary degree in 1963). In addition to her many mysteries and the New Zealand books, she penned two non-fiction guides to the theater: *A Play Toward: A Note on Play Production and Perspectives and The New Zealander* (1946) and *Visual Arts and Play Production* (1960).

Marsh's only collaboration was *The Nursing Home Murder*, which was written with a distinguished surgeon, Dr. Henry Jellett, one of Marsh's "Lamprey group."[5] *The Nursing Home Murder* was produced as a play with an amateur group and ironically, given her predilection for the theater, remains one of the rare stage presentations of Marsh's work.

On opening night the capacity crowd included many medical professionals. When the assistant surgeon dropped his glove during the on-stage "operation" and reached down to retrieve it, the audience roared. The genuine, experienced, registered surgical nurse drafted to play her usual role in the operating theater got so excited that she forgot this was a stage performance and clipped her retractors into the "patient's" flesh instead of the felt provided for her, and the actor had to endure agony while he was supposedly anesthetized. The actors playing the "doctors" could neither hear nor understand his muffled pleas for help!

The play generated so much realism that a professional actress from an English touring company in attendance fainted when the incision was uncovered, and had to be removed from the auditorium. Dr. Jellett, seated in the stalls, secreted a little ether to generate verisimilitude. To top it all off, one of the actors accidently ran a hypodermic needle into himself. Though successful, in spite of the first night disasters, the play was considered too close in tone to a popular American play, *Men in White*, to be staged professionally.

There were a handful of other stage performances of the mysteries. The Embassy Theatre at Hampstead produced a piece by Owen Howell based on *Surfeit of Lampreys*. Marsh reports that while the script was not bad, the production was too heavy-handed and failed to convey the Lamprey sprightliness. *False Scent* was another of her books that was adapted for the stage to no great acclaim, although the role of the aging actress must have been a choice one. In 1972 a version Marsh did of *Singing in the Shrouds* was produced as *Death Sails at Midnight*. *The Christmas Tree* (1962) is a play for juveniles which does not include Inspector Alleyn.

Her novels *were* well-received, however, and in 1978 she was honored with the Grand Master Award of the Mystery Writers of America. On the modest author's death at eighty-two, her March 1st obituary in *Time* nestled alongside those of Hurricane Jackson, Thelonius Monk, René Dubos, and, most appropriately, Lee Strasberg of the Actor's Studio.

Marsh's first love was always the stage. Earl Bargainnier reports on her activity as producer-director of the following Shakespearean plays: *Hamlet, Macbeth, Julius Caesar, Antony and Cleopatra, A Midsummer Night's Dream, Henry IV, Part I, Othello, King Lear, Twelfth Night*, and *Henry V*.[6] She also directed Pirandello's *Six Characters in Search of an Author*, and Shaw's *The Devil's Disciple*. Her Shakespearean offerings, originally produced during World War II, were reintroduced to the New Zealand stage after a twenty-year absence. Her University of Canterbury players were so adept that they were hired to tour New Zealand and Australia professionally, and it is to her 1949 student players that *Night at the Vulcan* is dedicated.

While it is clear that Marsh's personal satisfaction lay in the recognition she received for her theatrical work; her financial freedom was due entirely to the publication of her thirty-two detective novels. The success of her mysteries allowed her to do all those other things which gave

13

her the most pleasure: the books she wrote on play production and on her native New Zealand; her own adaptations
and plays; her close work with her beloved Shakespeare;
and, in general, the full and satisfying existence she led
with her family and friends.

The intertwining of her experience in the theater
with her writing gave her fiction a truly unique flavor.
From the personality of Inspector Alleyn to the structurally
irrelevant yet interesting asides, the world of the stage is
always present in the world of Marsh's novels.

How does Ngaio Marsh differ from other successful
authors of suspense and mystery fiction? While they all
deal with interesting characters, intricate plots filled with
adventure and suspense, large sprinklings of clues, "red
herrings," and witty dialogue, Marsh has used these devices
as a dramatist would, envisioning how the action and dialogue would look and sound on stage. It is only natural
that one who spent most of her life producing and directing
plays professionally would make use of her talent for dramatic pattern in other areas of endeavor. Marsh's innate
sense of what works dramatically (the "star turn," so to
speak) obviously enhanced her writing style significantly.

Not only is her fiction presented in dramatic terms,
it is also filled with asides and references to stage, film, ra-
dio, and television trivia. Alleyn is well-rounded, literate,
and an avid theater-goer. His friend Nigel Bathgate is a
drama critic. Personal names are often puns or plays on
names of dramatic characters, and many of Marsh's characters *are* actors. Shakespearean allusions and quotations
appear in every novel; some of the mysteries feature plots
which parallel those of well-known plays; and Marsh's final
mystery is set during a run of *Macbeth*.

Earl Bargainnier, in his discussion of the Marsh
novels most associated and involved with the theater, concludes:

> When she decided to combine her two
> careers in these novels, she did not, as
> Symons has noted, just use the theatre as a
> "puzzle box." Rather her experiences as ac-

tress, director, and producer enabled her to create a fully realized theatrical world, involving plot, characterization, and atmosphere, as well as setting. They also allowed her—in her own voice or through her characters—to make statements on the personalities of actors, the nature of theatrical pain and joy, the necessary fantasizing process itself, and, most of all, her deep love of the theatre, in spite of her recognition of its jealousies, pretensions, and eccentricities. Whatever one may think of a particular novel, one must admit that Marsh has been generally able to use the theatre as an integral element of her detective fiction.[7]

LeRoy Panek has outlined the following analysis of the dramatic structure of Marsh's novels. The early chapters build atmosphere and character. Then murder occurs. Routine police work fills the middle sections, featuring, in particular, the various forensic tests and interviews with suspects and witnesses. There is a recapitulation by one or another of the secondary characters—usually Nigel Bathgate or Fox—then a confrontation or reenactment of the crime which identifies the murderer, followed by an extremely short summary.[8]

Viewed in this manner, it is obvious that Marsh's plots closely parallel that of classical drama: protasis, epistasis, catastrophe. Because Marsh follows the Aristotelian pattern, we are never subjected to a long, rambling, often boring, explanation of the detective's thinking process. Her favorite manner of dénouement relies more on revealing the true character of the guilty party, the antagonist, and less on a regurgitation of the technicalities concerning the actual crime itself and how it was performed. Murders in Marsh, Panek further notes, occur most frequently in front of an audience—theater goers, members of a cult, guests at a reception, artists, or, in the case of the hospital novel, an operating room staff.[9]

Marsh's works and characters seem to have made an acceptable transition into the modern era with the filming of several of her books (*Dead Water* and *Death at the Bar*, for example) for the PBS television anthology, *Mystery!* The following study will analyze Marsh's novels in context with her love of the theater and its influence on her work. Inspector Alleyn and his co-stars, the characters who are actors, the many Shakespearean allusions, and the use of theatrical devices may all serve to point the way toward a more complete overview of the dramatic mysteries of Ngaio Marsh.

II.

A STAR IS BORN

Inspector Alleyn and His Supporting Cast

Roderick Alleyn is invariably the star of Marsh's shows, even when he comes on late in the performance or is in disguise. Professional theatrical people immediately recognize in him a "star quality," an expression which is often repeated in the novels. In *False Scent* an influential director is hushed by Alleyn's "effortless authority." Known for that quality himself, Timon Gantry at first blusters and then obeys as respectfully as though he was not accustomed to controlling a cast of stars. Martyne Tarne of *Night at the Vulcan*, though a fledgling actress herself, recognizes quality. Hearing Alleyn, "she decided that his voice was a royal blue of the clearest sort."[1]

In fact, most of the actors who come in contact with Alleyn feel an affinity with the policeman who understands their craft and the plays they perform. Peregrine Jay, in *Killer Dolphin*, feels that Alleyn knows Shakespearean scholarship and the plays better than he does, and he is a professional director and producer.[2] This is a detective who seems as natural on stage as off, and he always manages a grand entrance.

In *A Man Lay Dead* Marsh experimented with behaviors in her character, some of which were dropped but most of which remained constant. The early Alleyn has much of the supercilious priggishness of Lord Peter Wimsey, with a touch of Bulldog Drummond "hard-boiled" toughness. At one point he actually orders the villains to "Put 'em up, my poppets," in a particularly tortured hybrid of the two types of detective.[3] Marsh's hero is from the first, however, a star without an ego problem. As soon as he enters the case he befriends first one, then two, then three "suspects" as he clears them of suspicion—because he intuitively recognizes their innate goodness. Unlike some others of his ilk (Inspector Morse comes to mind), Alleyn's intuitions are invariably correct.

The first of Alleyn's suspects to become a friend is Nigel Bathgate, a gossip columnist and drama critic—and, like his mentor, a professional analyst of character. The journalist becomes Alleyn's assistant in this and later books. The actress Angela North, a fast and skillful driver, is clearly innocent, first on the basis of her genuine charm and secondly, because Nigel falls in love with her. Both are young, high-spirited, well-educated, and decidedly upper class, à la Agatha Christie's "Tuppence and Tommy." If their characters had continued throughout Marsh's novels, Roderick Alleyn would likely have evolved into quite a different character, more like Dorothy Sayers' Lord Peter Wimsey perhaps, and certainly less appealing.

Another of Alleyn's early confidants is Vassily, an old servant of Russian background who is arrested as a Bolshevik conspirator, then released into Alleyn's custody. Vassily becomes Alleyn's valet and remains, for a short time, as a fixture in his home.

Marsh establishes her detective early on as a man who is capable of correctly assessing character, an asset which means much more to Alleyn than motive when he is solving crime. His faith in his own ability to make such judgments allows him to form a crime-solving team, a "play company," if you will, and each member of his especially-chosen "cast" has an important role to play in the solution of the case. Alleyn does not perform wonders of mental brilliance on his own, as does Sherlock Holmes.

In Marsh's first novel, *A Man Lay Dead* the pattern is set: Angela understands what "Tunbridge B" means and is able to obtain a valuable love letter; Nigel takes on a dangerous job and is briefly tortured; Vassily proves a Russian conspiracy was *not* involved in this particular murder. Throughout Alleyn underplays his "star" quality. He usually appears after the other characters have come "on stage" and after the murder has been committed.

Wimsy "superciliousness" is far more characteristic of Alleyn than Drummond "toughness," a trait which can be considered a legacy from Dorothy Sayers and Agatha Christie and their "genteel" amateur detectives. A less than ideal quality which remains consistent throughout the novels is Alleyn's utter lack of objectiveness. Once he has gotten to know a character he tends to give that person a descriptive, sometimes unflattering, nickname—"Icy Florence" or "Ethel the Intelligent."

Alleyn is also guilty of teasing his cohorts mercilessly. When Nigel accuses him of being "affected" for complaining about his bad memory, Alleyn retaliates by threatening to tell about Nigel's ugly bedroom slippers and corn plasters. The fact of the matter is that Alleyn *is* downright dishonest in his "I've got a filthy memory" line. He carries a notebook around and when he is not writing information in it, he has Nigel taking notes. He remarks facetiously to Inspector Boys, "You've guessed my boyish secret. I've been given a murder to solve—aren't I a lucky little detective?"[4] He remains typically squeamish about murder. The body looks "beastly," he observes.

In spite of such foppish tendencies Alleyn obviously has the makings of a distinctive character in his initial foray in Marsh's first novel. Although he is aware of the "murder game" which has become so popular at society parties, he has not played it, he quips, since he does not like "busman's holidays." Alleyn is polite but no-nonsense, and expresses—as tactfully as any gentleman could—his displeasure that the corpse has been moved without his permission. He looks every inch the gentleman to Angela, "very tall, and lean," not smiling easily, dark-hair, grey eyes, detached, with an Oxonian voice.[5]

His appearance, in fact, is what is expected of a professional actor. He is handsome but not vain, prepossessing but not unctuous. In another novel, on being told that he is good-looking, he modestly jokes that his partner Fox raves about him and changes the subject. He is very good with young people, but when he can no longer deal with them, he turns them over to someone like Angela, who then becomes a confidante to extract further bits of information.

Marsh takes advantage of the fact that readers of detective fiction are familiar with other heroes by allowing Alleyn to make jokes about his fictional counterparts. He tells Nigel, who quickly becomes known as his "Watson," that he does not want "a tame half-wit to make him feel clever" and offers him "a percentage of the honour and glory."[6]

Nigel and the other people who help Alleyn in later cases are often wrong, but never stupid, and he praises them generously. Alleyn is not a solitary Sherlock Holmes, in spite of his frequent jibes about "Nigel the Watson." Alleyn's need to elude the CID leads him to confide as freely as he does with honest, intelligent, trustworthy people like Nigel and Angela who are sensible risk-takers. With tongue firmly in cheek he tells his friends, "I don't expect you to solve the mystery; I merely want you to tell me how clever I am, whether you think so or not."[7] Marsh never meant Alleyn to solve his problems alone.

Alleyn's background is fuzzy in the early novels. Impressed by Alleyn's elegant flat, Nigel assumes that this is a man who has private means that allow him to "sleuth for sleuthing's sake."[8] Eventually we learn that he has a brother, George, who has inherited the family title, a delightful and perceptive mother, a sister-in-law and niece, an Oxford education, and background in the diplomatic service that did not meet his needs as a life-long career.

Alleyn does not see policework as a romantic pursuit, nor as an escape from tradition: he is every bit the stickler for procedure. He has no sense of glamour in his work. He does it well, and finds enjoyment in the arts, especially in the theater, as Marsh emphasizes more and more in the later works. His Oxford background is evident in his good taste in all things from his flat to theatrical excellence.

His method for crime solution is to interview each person alone in a quiet room in order to hear each one's story as soon as possible after the crime and without others about to influence his witness's version of what happened. He also employs a reconstruction of the crime with everyone's presence accounted for. This becomes the play-within-the-novel which is so characteristic of Marsh's later works. Alleyn explains that

> ...there is often a moment in a case when a piece of one's mind, one's feeling, one's sense, knows the end while all the rest of the trained brains cuts this intuitive bit dead.[9]

Alleyn must combine the routine work of the skilled and disciplined policeman with the sensitivity of a man deeply involved with the arts. The best chance he has to do this is during the interviews and reconstructions when he becomes (like Marsh) a producer-director, casting and guiding his suspects skillfully. There are few spectacular scenes of violence depicted in this kind of approach. Perhaps because she had not yet decided exactly how she would present her new creation, and was unsure how her readers would react, Marsh interpolated scenes in which Nigel tackles a suspect and is tortured, and the Brotherhood behaves in typical cloak-and-dagger fashion. Alleyn was off to a good start in *A Man Lay Dead*, but his character, as yet, was only half formed.

Subsequent novels utilized plots wherein Alleyn would attend a theatrical production which culminates in an actual murder: *Enter A Murderer*; *Black as He's Painted*; *Light Thickens*; and a *Wreath for Rivera*, all feature variations on this same theme; *When In Rome* finds Alleyn with a tour group when two murders are committed. Alleyn takes to the stage regularly, as he interviews witnesses or directs reenactments; his knowledge of the theater plays a large role in his solutions to the crimes.

In Marsh's second novel, *Enter A Murderer*, Alleyn's first "theatrical" case begins when he and Nigel attend a suspense play starring one of Nigel's long-time good friends. It is the first of several such performances with Alleyn in attendance which will conclude with a murder. Alleyn sounds like a typical fan, when he admits: "I do love a crook play, I do....An actor in his dressing-room will thrill me to mincemeat. I shall sit and goggle at him, I promise you."10 But when Alleyn and Nigel go backstage, his point of view is that of an experienced theater person:

> They at once sensed the indescribable flavour of the working half of a theatre when the nightly show is coming on. The stage door opens into a little realm, strange or familiar, but always apart and shut in. The passage led directly on to the stage, which was dimly lit and smelt of dead scene paint, of fresh grease paint, of glue-size, and of dusty darkness, time out of mind the incense of the playhouse. A pack of scene flats leaned against the wall and a fireman leaned against the outer flat, which was painted to represent a section of a bookcase. A man in shirt sleeves and rubber-soled shoes ran distractedly round the back of the set. A boy carrying a bouquet of sweet peas disappeared into a brightly-lit entry on the right. The flats of the "set" vanished up into an opalescent haze. Beyond them, lit by shaded lamps, the furniture of a library mutely faced the reverse side of the curtain. From behind the curtain came the disturbing and profoundly exciting murmur of the audience, and the immemorial squall of tuning fiddle-strings.11

There are many such descriptions in Marsh's novels. Like the long explanations of whales and whaling in Herman Melville's *Moby Dick*, these vivid descriptions paint a picture of a world foreign to most readers, and bring it into perspective.

Alleyn knows the theater and its lore well. After Arthur Surbonadier has been shot (an exit of an actor) Alleyn faces down the powerful Mr. Saint, announcing:

> A drama is being produced which you do not control and in which you play a part that

may or may not be significant. To carry my
flight of fancy a bit farther, I may add that
the flat-footed old Law is stage manager,
producer, and critic. And I, Mr. Saint, in
the words of an old box-office success, "I,
my Lords, embody the law."[12]

He can see through the best of actors, too. As an
experienced critic, Alleyn can tell when people are putting
on acts. Miss Vaughan (with whom he becomes infatuated)
weeps "beautifully." Janet Emerald runs "through the
gamut of the emotions."[13] The killer gives a great performance of horror at being the first to "discover" Props'
body—which was not there anymore because Alleyn had set
a trap. Alleyn notes that "he was up against good acting,"
but no one outwits him.[14]

Like most criminal investigators, Alleyn himself is a
fairly competent actor. In the later novels he will perform
on his own stage. One recurring role he plays is that of the
absent-minded policeman with the "filthy memory" (a
"Columbo" type). Not only does he perform the routine
himself, he advises Angela to "pretend to be a good deal
sillier than you really are."[15] He deliberately underplays
his Holmesian encyclopedic knowledge in order to catch
people off guard.

In *When in Rome* he meets a young travel agent and
identifies him by name, Pace, and announces: "Some two
years ago. You were in the room for about three minutes;
during which time you gave me a piece of very handy information."[16] So much for the "filthy memory." He continues to play his tourist part well, until he assumes authority at the request of the Italian police. Then he becomes the
consummate professional.

In *Colour Scheme* Alleyn plays his role so well that
even the reader may not guess his true identity until the last
page. While acting the role of a middle-aged gentleman,
Septimus Falls, Alleyn is "bent forward at a wooden angle
and leaning heavily on his stick."[17] Alleyn fans should,
however, recognize Falls' bookishness, extreme courtesy,
knowledge of the theater, and his ability to philosophize

about Shakespeare. Falls has seen all the London productions for over ten years. Alleyn, as Falls, still retains his "star quality." Dikon, who is familiar with actors, observes: "He's got good appearance."[18] In order to solve the case, Falls (Alleyn) times the "Saint Crispin" speech that the actor, Gaunt, recites, in order to determine the killer's *modus operandi*.

In *Singing in the Shrouds*, Alleyn, in order to capture the psychopathic killer, boards the *Cape Farewell* as C. J. Broderick. Captain Bannerman, recognizing Alleyn's ability, devises a role for him which suits his aristocratic nature: he becomes a cousin of the ship line's chairman, on a diplomatic mission to Canberra.

Alleyn's most amusing extended "acting" performance takes place in *Spinsters in Jeopardy*. He is working undercover to infiltrate a cult for the French Sûreté, who have suggested several covers—antiquarian, drug addict, occult freak—but although he considers placing a story in the local newspaper: "Distinguished painter visits Côte d'Azur with obscure husband and child,"[19] he gains entrance to the cult's mansion instead by playing a Good Samaritan to an American traveler in need of an appendectomy. He is fluent in French (and many other languages, from his early days in the diplomatic corps), but he pretends not to understand what is being said, and thus gains a great deal of information. He allows the Children of the Sun to believe he is, among other things, a dabbler in the occult, an amateur poet, and a big game hunter! Playing dumb and naive is not an easy task for Alleyn, but he and his colleague, Raoul, manage to bumble their way into the forbidden ceremony as votaries. Poor *macho* Raoul gets star billing by replacing a beautiful young woman—high heels and all!

It should be emphasized that Alleyn never works alone to solve his cases. His two regular recurring "costars" are his partner, Inspector Edward "Teddy" Fox, and his wife, Agatha Troy Alleyn. Nigel Bathgate and Angela serve similarly as "Watsons" in *A Man Lay Dead*. testing ideas, gathering information, posing as communists, and even doing dangerous physical things. In later books police procedure becomes progressively more important. At first Nigel and Fox exist side by side, Nigel continuing to do what he had in the first novel. But Fox is a policeman, and eventually it is he who takes over the notetaking and offers professional observations.

Earl Bargannier refers to Fox as a "lovable" and "contrasting second lead to [Marsh's] star."[20] LeRoy Panek has already observed that Fox's role grows more prominent as Marsh puts greater and greater emphasis on routine policework and on Alleyn's sensitivity.

Fox's opening entrance to Marsh's stage has no drama. He is simply the "second plain clothes man" and Nigel takes notes. "Inspector" is his title and his first lines are based on wrong assumptions: "I reckon that's our man....He's just the type. Neurotic, highly strung sort of bloke."[21] Unlike Alleyn, he reveals his common background through his language and habit of jumping to conclusions based on preconceived ideas. He is good-natured, as diplomatic in his way as Alleyn is in his, here first reciting a line that is to become so characteristic that in one of the last novels Troy and Alleyn recite it in unison: "We'll have to get you in the force, sir."[22] But he soon proves his worth as Alleyn's "valued old one."[23] It is Fox who is assigned to interview the lower classes, the Beadle, the hirelings, and dressers. Although he is perfectly at ease with Dulcie Deamer and hosts of cooks and ladies' maids, Fox is bashful around women and worshipful around the leading lady, Miss Vaughan.

Wherever they work Alleyn sends Fox to interview the female servants. His success, Alleyn teases, is due to his "unbridled body urge."[24] When the "chief" enters during an interview, the lower classes stiffen. Alleyn steps aside to watch since "Fox's technique on the working side of the green baize doors was legendary at the Yard."[25] Fox is genial, praises people, speaks French with the chef, and suggests that statements made to him will free them from suspicion. Alleyn winces at the last part, but admires his partner's routine. In *Hand in Glove* Alleyn admits that Fox reminds him of a reliable sheepdog as he rounds up the household staff. Fox is, however, capable of enthralling an aristocratic audience too, as he does in *Death of a Peer*. Alleyn finds the Lampreys grouped around him while Fox holds forth with "the air of a successful *raconteur*."[26]

Physically, Fox is a middle-aged man with bright eyes, large and imposing, a fellow who looks every inch of his six feet the policeman. In *Light Thickens* he is described as "the regular, old-style, plainclothesman: grizzled, amiable and implacable."[27] Troy holds that "Mr. Fox was a cross between a bear and a baby and exhibited the most pleasing traits of both creatures."[28] Alleyn finds something very comforting about Fox sitting next to him taking notes. He is always efficient, scrupulously recording everything of importance. He is never ill, a fact that squelches his romance with Nurse Kettle in *Scales of Justice*. To comfort him Alleyn observes that she needs someone to care for and Fox does not need help. Fox remains a bachelor to the end, totally centered on his career. In *False Scent* Alleyn decides that "his arrival at any scene of disturbance has the effect of a large and almost silent vacuum cleaner."[29]

Fox works competently and independently, is an expert on drugs, and has successfully managed an AC (arson case) on his own. In *Last Ditch* we learn that Fox has something of a photographic memory, and is capable of remembering names after a first introduction. In *Death in a White Tie* he worries about Alleyn who is under the double pressure of tracking down a friend's killer while trying to win Troy. Fox takes charge, lending support and advice to Alleyn when the case takes on a personal urgency. "You'll do no good if you try and work it on your nerves," Fox advises,[30] trying to assuage his friend's guilt over the death of Lord Robert Gospell.

> Fox, completely at his ease, stood like a rock in the middle of the room. He appeared to be lost in a mild abstraction but he could have gone away and described the library with the accuracy of an expert far-gone in Pelmanism.[31]

Fox is adept at "disappearing" into the woodwork. He first clears his throat, retires into a "self-made obscurity," takes out his notebook and then listens "with his customary air; raised brows, pursed lips, and a hint of catarrhal breathing."32 It is a remarkable act of self-effacement.

Fox functions as a teacher for Sergeant Plank in *Last Ditch*, telling him that a policeman's life is a lonely one, cut off from others whenever there is a major crime. At one point, as they sit in a bar collecting gossip from the locals, Plank asks Alleyn to tell about his experience with a child killer. Later, Fox tells Plank never to do that, since reminding people of their jobs cuts off the flow of information. He also warns younger policemen never to assume guilt on the basis of appearances, since character typing can lead a policeman too far from the truth. He's right: Some of Marsh's most disgusting human beings, like Charmless Claude of *Grave Mistake*, are innocent of the major crime.

From the third book on Fox begins to think like Alleyn. Knowing that Alleyn wants Dr. Roberts out of the operating theater, Fox arranges for him to receive a telephone call. He too can play a role convincingly. In *The Nursing Home Murder* he appears as a middle-aged toothless man who exudes gloom and outrage, laughing in such a sinister manner that he frightens Nigel and Angela. His "diabolical French" betrays him at last. The "Brer Fox" and "Foxkin" nicknames are first mentioned in *Death in Ecstasy* and remain. His role is often to tell others that Alleyn is a real aristocrat, to avoid anyone's thinking that he is a fake, and to make certain that people know how important he is.

Alleyn shares more than his office with Fox. In *Scales of Justice* Marsh describes the two men contemplating each other "with the absent-minded habit of long association."33 In *Vintage Murder* Alleyn thinks of Fox and how he never has to show off for his "large and slow and innocently straight-forward" partner.34 The two are interlocking parts of a perfect working team who think alike when it comes to procedures, no matter how different they are in appearance, education, family background, and personality.

Though Alleyn often seems silly in his pursuit of Troy, when Fox is poisoned in *Death at the Bar* his concern is utterly convincing. His face tells Miss Darragh that something disastrous has happened. His diplomacy fails him as he shouts orders for everyone to remain where they are. His whole energy goes into the work of resuscitating Fox. Alleyn's glass of sherry has not been touched; it is poor Fox who must "neatly and proficiently [make] use of the basin."[35] "Very inconvenient," says Fox. "Sorry," Alleyn responds, "Fox, my dear old thing."[36] Since these are classic detective stories, there is no chance for Fox to throw himself in front of Alleyn to save him from death. But Marsh's readers can tell that he would.

Although Fox is competent and skilled, he is funny enough to provide a necessary comic relief to the serious topic of murder. There is a nice picture of the two senior detectives practicing their old skills of shadowing a suspect in *Black as He's Painted*. Fox advises Alleyn to scream if too frightened by Trixie, the over-sexed barmaid in *Death of a Fool*. In *Hand in Glove* he wryly observes that his staff has extracted enough soil from the excavation and turkish tobacco from Mr. Period's cigarettes to satisfy "a blind juryman in a total eclipse."[37] He is neither as lightning quick nor as brilliant as his chief, but he has a "masterly command of the totally unexpected" that proves useful.[38] His respect for the upper classes, his tendency to "enthrall" pub audiences with tales of Alleyn's adventures, and his attempts to learn and use French from the BBC (with tutoring promised from Miss Emily Pride in *Dead Water*) all provide enough "light touches" to prevent a reader from growing bored.

Since Marsh had been exposed to comic relief in her study of Shakespeare, It is tempting to compare Fox's character with those of Falstaff and Dogberry (although Fox is never depicted as being stupid, except, perhaps, by Lord Pastern). Unlike Falstaff, Fox brags only about his distinguished partner's prowess. Nor is he given to cowardice, trickery, or over-indulgence.

Alleyn, in fact, refers to Fox's "blameless bed" on several occasions. Fox, a bachelor, disapproves of loose women, improper social behavior, and most deviations from the status quo. In *Death in Ecstasy*, for example, he is offended by nude statues and talk of gay lovers. He is a strong traditionalist. In *Scales of Justice* he announces that "The Rape of Lucrece" should be on the police list. In *Artists in Crime* he is scandalized by the Bohemian life style, and by artists in general (although he soon learns that even Bohemians can be stodgy). In spite of his misgivings, he finds the artist Agatha Troy to be a very pleasant person. He becomes friends with both Lady Alleyn (Alleyn's mother) and Troy, and he develops a close relationship with Ricky Alleyn, his godson. Fox is a man of simple tastes. He does not put on airs, and will not even attend a dinner party because it would be

> ...an affected kind of way for me to act....I never get a black coat or boiled shirt on my back except at the Lodge meeting and when I'm on a night-club job. The Colonel would only think I was trying to put myself in a place where I don't belong.[39]

Fox is a long way from being a power-hungry scoundrel like Falstaff.

Fox allows Alleyn to get in and out of sticky situations without too much loss of dignity. His nature blends a taste for propriety with slapstick humor, in much the same way Alleyn's aristocratic background contrasts rather agreeably with his facetiousness. In fact the two men balance each other out well, their very incongruity lending humor to otherwise serious situations. They are embarrassed when Sonia Orrincourt discovers them searching her room in *Final Curtain* and becomes irate. Fox must mention Alleyn's title to convince her they have official business there; however, she breaks into laughter when she realizes that the dignitary's wife is involved in the case. In the same book the two of them sit down to play "Happy Families" with a problem child (who cheats). Their craziest moment comes in *Grave Mistake* when an attractive but imposing nurse causes them to act incongruously. Alleyn has entered a curtained alcove to examine its contents. Suddenly Sister Jackson appears and Fox,

> ...with a movement surprisingly nippy for one of his bulk, joined his superior in the alcove.

They turn off the flashlight, then wonder why they are hiding. "You're bulging the curtain," Alleyn complains. When Sister Jackson discovers them and screams, Alleyn shines the flashlight full in her face and says, "Good morning." When she asks shakily what they are doing there, he responds, "Routine procedure. Don't give it another thought."[40]

Although this scene is humorous, it takes place during their discovery that Sybil Foster has been murdered. Still, they find it hard to keep a straight face whenever they think of Sister Jackson's broom closet. Fox even adopts a pronounced diction when he announces Bailey and Thompson are "like they say in theatrical circles, below and awaiting your pleasure." "Admit them," responds Alleyn.[41] Their work may be routine, but these two obviously enjoy their time together.

Fox is not present when Alleyn's adventures occur abroad—in *Colour Scheme*, *Vintage Murder*, *Died in the Wool*, *Photo Finish*, and *Spinsters in Jeopardy*—but Alleyn keeps him informed, laments his absence, or asks him to do some research or routine legwork back at the Yard.

Although Miss Pride accuses him of mutilating French pronunciation, and George Pastern complains that he is a terrible jazz pianist, Fox otherwise is a model of proficiency. When Lord Pastern calls Fox a "great hamfisted ass of a chap" for telling him that he is acting foolishly, Alleyn returns politely that Fox is "an extremely efficient officer and should have had his promotion long ago."[42] Later Lord Pastern wonders if he could become a policeman too and Miss Pride takes Fox on as a French student. Fox has quietly winning ways.

In fact, Fox's role as part foil and part straight man, makes him always the ideal colleague, reliable and efficient. Had Marsh developed Mike Lamprey, for instance, into Alleyn's partner, their similarities would not have allowed for the wide range of people and situations touched by the interesting combination of the handsome charming aristocrat and the staid, comfortable-looking common man. With Fox at his side to do the hard drudgery of routine work, yet able to cope with the occasional dangerous confrontation, Alleyn no longer has need of assistants like Angela and Nigel.

Just as Fox is the perfect partner for Alleyn, so Troy is the perfect wife. Marsh has written about Agatha Troy Alleyn in *Murder, Ink*, explaining that her own interest in painting led to Troy's creation in the sixth book, and to the artistic *milieu* in which Alleyn finds himself because of Troy.

Marsh's agent was unsure about her introduction of a love interest into the novels, but Marsh chose wisely. With an ideal mate at home, Alleyn can be the object of outrageous flirtations by gorgeous actresses as well as a knowledgable purveyor of wisdom to young women in love, without risking unseemly involvement himself. Troy is often described as the "elegant lady" with Alleyn. She comes across as an absent-minded, shy, witty woman with thin face and hands, and short dark hair. She is a fine painter with an international reputation and her works hang in some of the great private collections. Not surprisingly, one of her best is a portrait of her husband painted during their initial shipboard romance.

Troy, although an artist, is not an actress, and Alleyn never requires that role of her. Alleyn is capable of finding needed information on his own, and Troy is not asked to help. In fact, he has stated that he would rather quit his job and start a school for detectives than to interfere with her work. Thus Troy never has to be anyone but herself.

Troy is reticent, though perfectly capable of dealing with men who flirt with her. She attends the theater with her husband in *Killer Dolphin* and *Light Thickens* and visits a night club with him in *A Wreath for Rivera*, when she simply goes off to bed following the murder! She has a good reason we discover; Alleyn informs Fox that he is going to be a godfather when they freshen up the next morning!

In *Dead Water* and *Last Ditch* Troy visits her injured husband and son in hospitals, but plays no major role other than as comforter and supporter. She never complains about the danger Alleyn finds himself in, nor the long hours he works, although she occasionally grumbles about interrupted vacation time, as for example in *Dead Water* and *Death and the Dancing Footman*. In the latter novel she is painting the handsome Father Copeland whom Alleyn had met in *Overture to Death*. As Alleyn is cleaning her paints (his particular assignment while she works) a call for help comes during a raging blizzard. While Alleyn goes over reasons why he needn't interfere in other policemen's assignments, Troy is already upstairs packing his bag.

Artists in Crime and *Death in a White Tie* (to which Marsh jokingly referred as "The Siege of Troy") cover Alleyn's courtship of Troy. When he first sees her, Alleyn is being pursued by a beautiful young woman who looks like a film star, but he prefers the distinctive lady whose painting style he immediately recognizes. In a letter to a friend Troy introduces the cast of the murder story, showing the sharp eye that is to become a great help to her future husband. her first words are "Damn" and "Blast," interesting since Alleyn rarely curses, his favorite outbursts being "Bloody" and "Bastard."

In *Death in a White Tie* Alleyn wins Troy's sympathy because they share affection for the victim. Lady Alleyn thinks Troy would make a wonderful daughter-in-law, but is clever enough to keep her ideas to herself (and the reader). Alleyn declares his love for Troy, complaining that she makes it hard for him to concentrate on solving crimes. The intelligent and perceptive Troy, however, does not want him to confuse pity, gratitude or even respect with love, and holds back. Troy is very much afraid of losing her independence.

However, Alleyn is not only gone a lot of the time on long trips (which allows her a great deal of freedom), he is a genuine feminist who does not envision his wife as a mere appendage. He is accustomed to dealing with talented and powerful women, including his own mother, and he enthusiastically encourages Troy to put her career first. He graciously accepts the role of "paint-cleaner" and straightener of household disarray, and finds his wife's tendency toward messiness appealing (Troy is invariably smudged with paint.)

In return, Troy is a sympathetic listener who (like Nigel) provides yet another outside point of view. When Troy and Alleyn are separated during the war, his letters to her emphasize how much he misses her; he sees the people and landscapes about him through her eyes—just as if she were with him. At times he tries out his ideas on her, and tests his investigative theories with her—even at a distance. Thus she is actively engaged in his work, and acting as his "Watson," from their London flat. In *Singing in the Shrouds* he summarizes all the facts in letters to her, and asks if she can spot any obvious links in the crimes. Troy is an objective observer—partially because she doesn't read crime fiction (a trait she shares with Fox—who does not read them because they are so "unrealistic").

Final Curtain is the first novel to begin with Troy working on a portrait at the time someone is killed. Though natural death is the common assumption, her subject has actually been murdered. Troy's memory of a conversation she had with Sir Henry Ancred provides the necessary clue, and her descriptions and sketches of the people staying at Ancreton help her husband prepare for his interviews.

Troy, in this novel, chooses to become actively involved in Alleyn's work. In fact, this is the first novel in which she has a large part. As the artist of the portrait unveiled in a theater on the momentous occasion of Sir Henry's birthday, she "found herself suddenly projected into a star role."[43] To make things even more interesting, it is quite clear that the Alleyns' relationship is being redefined following the nearly four year separation early in their marriage, when both were assigned to war work. Troy has been apprehensive that Alleyn's absence "will drop like a curtain between their understanding of each other."[44]

In *Spinsters in Jeopardy* while her husband is actively pursuing a drug ring and a murderer, her son is kidnapped, allowing Troy to be, above all, in this novel, a worried mother. Troy is immediately recognized in the town where she goes to visit her cousin, P. E. Garbel; even if she were not already a famous artist known by many people, the presence in the area of another artist who has studied with her would have given her away. Troy misses the clues in her fussy cousin's chatty postcards, which contain odd pleas to Alleyn to come visit her.

A Clutch of Constables finds Troy taking a pleasure inland river cruise aboard the *Zodiac* while Alleyn is on assignment in America, and Ricky is in Grenoble. London is hot and empty and, following her one-woman show in New York and Paris, Troy is ready for a five-day step out of time. She finds, however, that she has stepped *into* an art forgery ring instead. Although Troy is the featured player in this novel, Alleyn shows up to take her ashore during the investigation, fortunately, since nearly everyone on the boat is dangerous. Troy visits some police stations while on shore, allowing Marsh a chance to make the following comments on policemen and their work:

> They were men who, day in, day out, worked in an atmosphere of intense hostility. They were, they would have said, without illusions and, unless a built-in skepticism by definition includes a degree of illusion, she supposed they were right. Some of them, she thought, had retained a kind of basic compassion; they were shocked by certain crimes and angered by others. They honestly saw themselves as guardians of the peace, however disillusioned they might be as to the character of the beings they protected....Many of them, like Fox, were of a

very kindly disposition, yet as Alleyn once
said of them, if pity entered far into the
hunter his occupation was gone. And he had
quoted Mark Antony who talked about "pity
choked with custom of fell deeds."[45]

Troy understands and is sympathetic with that world—but
she remains outside of it.

Another portrait involves her in the role of a witness
in *Tied Up in Tinsel*. She overhears conversations, gets to
know all the suspects, and endures Cressida Tottenham's
flirting with Alleyn. Although Cressida is gorgeous, Troy
knows that there is no depth to the woman and makes it
clear to Cressida's doting fiancé that she will not do his
future wife's portrait as a companion piece to the one she is
painting of him. She must find strength of character and
basic goodness in people in order to do her best work. Although she has no real role in solving the crime, her husband's investigations bear out her initial impressions. Similarly in *Black as He's Painted* she does a portrait of the
Boomer, her husband's old school friend. Though the constant danger of assassination lurks, Troy is too delighted
with her wonderful model to worry much about it.

Another ideal subject is Isabella Sommita, the opera
diva in *Photo Finish*, and in this novel the presence of both
Troy and Alleyn is required for their respective professional
skills. Troy helps comfort Rupert Bartholomew and knows
when to disappear so that the two men can talk. Troy
comes as close as she ever does, in this novel, to playing a
"housewifely" role which is atypical of her. Perpetually
dishevelled and paint-bespattered, Troy is certainly no
housekeeper; but she and the doctor make up the beds in
the luxury lodge belonging to the multi-millionaire Reece,
while everyone else is busy. She is annoyed, Alleyn can
tell, because she has a tendency to get "all joky" in such
circumstances.[46]

Other than Katti Bostock and the Bathgates, Troy
has no close personal friends, although she fits comfortably
into whatever social *milieu* she finds herself. She takes on
promising students, and interviews potential artists in her

home. Unlike an actress with a heavy rehearsal and performance schedule, Troy always seems to be home and
cheerful whenever Alleyn needs someone to listen to him,
and, from the first, she is the ideally perceptive listener.

Alleyn himself knows everyone up to and including
the Prime Minister; he has a mother, a brother, sister-in-
law, and niece, as well as close personal friends, like Nigel
and Angela Bathgate and their child. The competent Bailey
and Thompson are always there to fill in his working team
with camera and finger-printing expertise, and local policemen are all glad of his gracious assistance. Still, once
they are introduced, his main supporting actors are Fox and
Troy, who as partner and wife, play the most important
parts in the protagonist's life and work.

III.

ALL THE WORLD'S A STAGE

THE DRAMATIS PERSONAE IN MARSH'S FICTION

Alleyn's stage is full of actors, actresses, and people of the theater. *Enter a Murderer, Colour Scheme, False Scent, Final Curtain, Photo Finish, Light Thickens, Vintage Murder, Night at the Vulcan,* and *Killer Dolphin* all include high-quality professional actors at the center of the plot, while amateur or beginning performers and productions appear in *Death of a Peer, Dead Water, Death at the Bar, Grave Mistake, Overture to Death, Tied Up in Tinsel,* and *A Wreath for Rivera* (see Appendices I and II).

In *Enter a Murderer* Alleyn meets his first genuine actor in a backstage dressing room and begins a career-long fascination with the theater. Before long his natural good sense has allowed him to analyze the behavior of these unique professionals. Felix Gardener, Nigel Bathgate's school friend, has an "elusive quality of distinction,"[1] without being too handsome to be true. Felix manages, in fact, not to be too much of anything.

> He was tall, carried himself beautifully, but not too much like a showman, and he had a really delightful speaking voice, light but resonant. He was said by women to have "It"; by men to be a very decent fellow; and by critics to be an actor of outstanding ability.[2]

Alleyn quickly meets a number of Felix's colleagues. The second actor is J. Barclay Crammer, a character actor whom people recognize but do not get excited about.

37

Arthur Surbonadier took the role for which he had been scheduled—a role that would have given Crammer star billing. The "unmistakable gust of alcohol" that precedes the unpleasant Surbonadier prepares the reader for his early demise.[3] Felix explains that Surbonadier resents him for being the lead in the play. Thus Alleyn is initiated into the jealousies that arise from competition for choice theatrical roles. Before long he also learns of the more serious rivalry between the two actors over the leading actress, Stephanie Vaughan. When Gardener introduces her, Alleyn immediately is aware of her aggressiveness. She comes close, in fact, to sweeping the inspector off his feet:

> She received them with much gaiety, gave them cigarettes and dealt out her charm lavishly, with perhaps an extra libation for Gardener and a hint, thought Nigel, of something more subtly challenging in her manner toward Inspector Alleyn. Even with blue grease on her eyelids and scarlet grease on her nostrils, she was a very lovely woman, with beautifully groomed hair, enormous eyes, and a heart-shaped face. Her three-cornered smile was famous.[4]

The other actress Alleyn meets backstage, Susan Max, is simply "an elderly woman," though she turns out to be someone Alleyn admires as a person and a performer.

After the murder Alleyn observes the actors with the eye of a critic. When Miss Vaughan leaves, it is with "touching dignity," allowing herself to be led off stage and shuddering at her last look at the corpse. Wryly Alleyn observes: "Lovely exit, wasn't it?"[5]

Alleyn also recognizes that Jacob Saint has an off-stage role. When he comforts his mistress, actress Janet Emerald, he does so in his "best theatre-magnate manner."[6] An actor early in his career, Saint has become the wealthy proprietor of the Unicorn Theatre. Now his act is that of an entrepreneur who seems to be playing his own character, a caricature of the power behind the actors.

"Saint" in fact is no longer plain Jacob Simes, as his nephew is no longer Arthur Simes. Both have taken on roles with their new names, but both are still petty, dishonest men who will stop at nothing to be in control. Jacob is perceptive, and recognizes the ability of professional actors to perform their roles in everyday life as well, and so informs Surbonadier in no uncertain terms, when the actor asks him to fire Gardener and give him the leading part:

"Spoken deliberately—comes down-stage slowly. Quite the little actor, aren't you?"[7]

In fact stage directions play an integral role in the action because of the many performances taking place both on *and off* stage. Even Nigel writes in brackets as he takes shorthand notes: "Noise of theatre magnate sitting down."[8]

It does not take Alleyn long to decide that "We're up against good acting."[9] When he interviews Stephanie Vaughan, she weeps "not noisily or with ugly distortions of her face, but beautifully."[10] She conveys an image of the helpless female, which is not exactly true. Later on the actors give their various interpretations of "playing the part" at an inquest:

Barclay Crammer gave a good all-round performance of a heart-broken gentleman of the old school. Janet Emerald achieved the feat known to leading ladies as "running through the gamut of the emotions." Asked to account for the striking discrepancies between her statement and those of Miss Max and the stage manager, she wept unfeignedly and said her heart was broken. The coroner stared at her coldly, and told her she was an unsatisfactory witness. Miss Deamer was youthfully sincere, and used a voice with an effective little broken gasp. Her evidence was supremely irrelevant.[11]

Even at the reconstruction of the crime the actors perform. Janet Emerald walks

> ...with the gait she used in the provinces for the last act of *Madam X*. Dulcie Deamer followed, expressing tragic bewilderment.... Howard Melville and J. Barclay Crammer delayed their entrance and made it arm-in-arm with heads held high, like French aristocrats approaching the tumbrels.[12]

But once on stage in their true environment they are real. After Alleyn has trapped the killer he admits that he had been skeptical of everyone—so he can discover the truth in spite of their "sincere" performances. The killer had tried to convince Alleyn that he was the only *genuine* person among a crew of posturing actors. At the end of this second mystery, Alleyn has learned how to evaluate the behavior of actors very competently.

Although Geoffrey Gaunt, in *Colour Scheme*, is painted satirically, the man is a genuine talent. He tells of his experience of reading the "Eve of Crispin" speech from *Henry V* as a child and how he was caught up in its magic so that he knew, as a boy, he had to become a Shakespearean actor. At the Maori party Gaunt appears last on the program and does speeches from *Macbeth* and *Henry V*, aware that "Friends, Romans, Countrymen" may be the only Shakespeare known to his audience. Marsh comments:

> ...an audience meant only one thing to him: it was a single entity that must fall in love with him, and, as a corollary, with Shakespeare.[13]

The female version of the egotistical actor appears in *False Scent*. The novel begins with actress, and victim-to-be, Mary Bellamy fantasizing about her loving public's response to her funeral (sometime in the future). "She was loved by all and inspired love in others, her colleagues, friends, and, of course, her husband." Her fantasy ends with a funeral as grand as she could wish for—and a reporter wondering what Mary's husband's name is.

Mary is about to star in a new play written especially for her by her ward, Richard Dakers. It's her fiftieth birthday and—while she feels confident that she still looks wonderful without makeup—she hopes no one can guess her true age. After twenty years of marriage she no longer cares for her husband who, at sixty, is florid from heart disease, pot-bellied, and unattractive and unglamorous in general. Mary is deceiving herself into believing that she is still young and beautiful enough to play her favorite leading commedienne roles. She dons her new gown and poses in the bright sunlight, unaware that she is not showing herself off to best advantage.

> She had made an entrance, comic-provocative, skillfully French-farcical. She had no notion at all of the disservice she had done herself. [14]

Mary has earned her reputation through hard work and genuine talent, but the high temperament for which many actors are known has become pathological in her. When she learns that her supporting actress has become a star in her own play and that her personal designer has agreed to "do" her new rival's wardrobe, Mary becomes a "Delphic fury" and threatens publicly to ruin both—which as controller of the theater's stock she can do.

Worse yet, Mary is insanely jealous of her ward Richard's beautiful actress friend who has been given the lead role in a new play by Richard—*Husbandry in Heaven*—which is not even a comedy! For his whole career Richard has been writing comedies exclusively for Mary out of loyalty to her for taking him in as a baby. He is totally unaware that Mary in reality is his mother and that a "friend of the family" who is always nearby is his real father. There are "red herrings" a-plenty when Mary meets her sudden unexpected demise.

Upon receiving news of the volatile actress's suspicious death, Alleyn reports cynically as he prepares to enter the case:

> A lady of the theatre...appears to have looked upon herself as a common or garden pest and sprayed herself out of this world. She was mistaken as far as her acting was concerned. Miss Mary Bellamy. A comedienne of the naughty darling school and not a beginner.[15]

In *Final Curtain* Troy is called on to do a portrait of Sir Henry Ancred, a seventy-five year old theatrical giant, costumed in his role as Macbeth. His son, Thomas, a producer associated with the Unicorn Theatre tells Troy:

> He is quite good, of course, though a little creaky at times, don't you feel? And then, all those mannerisms! He can't play an emotional bit, you know, without sucking in his breath rather loudly. But he really is good in a magnificent Mrs. Beeton sort of way. A recipe for everything and only the best ingredients used.[16]

Since an ungrateful nation has failed to provide Ancred with a commissioned portrait, it is only appropriate to have "the great British actor painted by the great British artist." Troy, on furlough from war work because of a painful carbuncle and eager to see her husband who is to return from duty after three years, finds herself swept into the commission against her wishes. Appropriately, the intended backdrop for the portrait is one she herself had designed for the production in which Sir Henry starred. Thomas practically blackmails her into doing the portrait by setting the scene up thusly:

> "He speaks the Shakespearean lines as an actor would, knowing their value." He had

tried acting himself and could appreciate his father's skill.

"It's red, a Paul Veronese-ish red, dark but clear, with a smoky overcloak. We've got a miniature theatre in Ancreton, you know. I brought down the original backdrop for one of the inset scenes and hung it. It's quite a coincidence...that you did the original designs for that production? Of course you remember the one I mean. It's very simple. A boldly distorted castle form seen in silhouette. He dressed himself and stood in front of it, resting his claymore with his head, stood, as if listening: 'Good things of day begin to droop and drowse,' do you remember?"

Troy remembered that line very well. It was strange that he should have recalled it; for Alleyn was fond of telling her how, in the small hours of a stormy morning, a constable on night duty had once quoted it to him.[17]

Sir Henry is still handsome and a great man with the ladies. Impressed by Troy's beauty as well as her reputation, Sir Henry shows her his three albums of theatrical photos. Though besotted by a beautiful young chorus girl his family barely tolerates, Sir Henry is an appealing gentleman. Troy is impressed by him and comes to know him as a vulnerable, intelligent man. At one point she apologizes for forgetting that he would tire, and the following conversation ensues:

"One also remembers....I have been remembering my lines. I played the part first in 1904."
"It's a wonderful role."

She had seen him in *Macbeth* five years before and had been moved....

"I've played it six times and always to
enormous business. It hasn't been an unlucky piece for me...."

Troy asks him about the *Macbeth* superstition, the unlucki-
ness associated with quoting from the play. It has, hasn't
it, been unlucky for others?

"There's always a heavy feeling offstage
during performances. People are nervy....
You can't escape the feeling. But the piece
has never been unlucky for me....If it were
otherwise, should I have chosen this role for
my portrait? Assuredly not!"[18]

Sir Henry takes his glasses out to look at what Troy
has done and Troy is amused to see "Macbeth with glasses
perched on his nose [stare] solemnly at his own portrait."[19]
He adjusts his cloak, draws himself up and utters:

"Off, ye lendings! I must change!" His
voice, as though husbanded for this one
flourish boomed through the empty theatre.
"Well, may you see things well done
there: adieu!
"Lest our old robes sit easier than our
new!...
"...God's benison go with you," said
Troy, luckily remembering the line. [He
crosses himself and exits.][20]

When the actor dies, the assumption is that his in-
sistence on drinking and eating what is bad for his gastroenteritis has done him in, but when the suspicion of
murder arises, Troy is already involved enough to assist
Alleyn in finding the murderer. In spite of his overly emotional nature and his apparently illicit affair, Sir Henry is a
decent, sensitive man whom Troy had admired. Even his
love attachment is not overly sordid, as the allusion to
Abishag the Shunammite, attendant to David in his old age,

and the formal engagement imply. He deserves the Alleyns' time and attention.

Sir Henry's fiancée, Sonia Orrincourt, is a bad actress who is soon cast in the role of murderess by Henry's family. She has not one ounce of class to match her astonishing beauty. Troy and Fenella, however, do not share the seemingly universal dislike for this young woman and, since Troy and young people in love are the two things Alleyn trusts most, he continues to probe until it becomes clear that Sonia's only guilt is her lack of theatrical skill. She does not even have the talent to conceal her glee at the pranks she and Cedric Ancred have been playing (though at first Troy thinks Sonia is suffering from asthma when she sees her shoulders shake after she purchases something which causes a bulge in her pocket). It takes a better actress than Sonia to perform murder in Marsh's books.

The Ancreds are a theatrical family, though no one is as successful as the patriarch. Thomas, acknowledging his lack of talent in the acting department, has become, instead, a producer. His skill at manipulating people and his practical nature (which show themselves when he courts the pretty teacher of children with special needs) suggest that he is more talented than people might assume. His sister, Desdemona is the most interesting of the family professionals. Even though her skill is lacking, she succeeds because she is so attractive. Marsh sums up the lady as:

> ...a good emotional actress, difficult to place as she has a knack of cracking the seams of the brittle, slickly drawn roles for which West-End managements, addled by her beauty, occasionally cast her. She has become attached to a Group and appears in pieces written by two surrealists, uttering her lines in such a heart-rendering manner that they seem, even to Desdemona herself, to be fraught with significance.[21]

And that is Marsh's view of experimental theater and the stereotypical "dumb" actress. Marsh, in this novel alone, portrays several levels of theatrical performance, from pretty but shallow show girl to skilled and revered Shakespearean actor.

In *Photo Finish* the main player is an opera *diva*—a performer both on and off the stage. Isabella Sommita's breath control is flawless and controlled, but her disposition is not:

> Offstage when moved by one of her not infrequent rages, La Sommita's bosom would heave with the best of them.[22]

At one point she is caught by the phantom photographer who has been tormenting her. Her jaw has dropped; her left eye has slewed, a mannerism of her fury; and the resultant photograph has the effect of "a gargoyle at the dentist's: an infuriated gargoyle."[23] Beautiful and talented, La Sommita does not want this kind of publicity and so the man assumed to be her lover, Montague Reece, requests that Troy do a portrait with Alleyn alongside acting as a bodyguard to protect the singer from her strange tormentor who signs himself "Strix."

Photo Finish is another satiric portrayal of a star. La Sommita, although technically the greatest soprano of her time, is musically illiterate. Her total lack of judgment and overwhelming egotism lead her to perform an opera written by her young lover which shows off her virtuosity at the expense of the other performers. Unfortunately, the opera is generally awful—"Menotti and soda water," her voice coach calls it—and leads to great suffering for the naive Rupert Bartholomew. La Sommita is a caricature (strikingly like Maria Callas) of the operatic *diva* who has won international fame for her flamboyant lifestyle, passionate relationships, and attachment to a multimillionaire.

The actors who appear in *Light Thickens* are an appealing lot, very much like the ensemble players in a production who do not, generally, appear as stars. As a matter of fact, *Light Thickens* is probably the best portrait of a working theatrical company which Marsh has produced, replete with management decisions, publicity problems, and a great deal of information about the technical preparation of a production. Alleyn's role is minimal and, in fact, the major breakthrough in solving the crime comes from young Robin Jay's accurate observation as revealed when he is playing with his brother and William Smith. The cast members of the play become absorbed in the powerful aura:

> It was as though each actor continued in
> an assumed character, and no other reality
> existed.[24]

Even with pranks, superstitious gossip, a romantic triangle, and Bruce's hatred for the innocent boy because of his father's crime, the production is ideal. The critic whose opinion people most value calls it "the best *Macbeth* since Olivier."

The company assembles early in the book: There are nineteen people in the cast, many of whom are mentioned only in passing. Simon Morten is Macduff, six-foot-two, dark, curly black hair, a wonderful voice, and a good physique—too good to be true, he is an ideal actor for Peregrine Jay. Bruce Barrabell has a beautiful voice too, a slight, light-haired contrast as Banquo. He holds a grudge against the child actor in the production. His "hobby horse" is politics. Not only has he toured Russia with the Leftist Players, he is the local representative of the Red Fellowship of which it is said:

> Nobody seemed to know what it wanted
> except that it didn't want anything that was
> established or that made money in the the-
> atre.

On the other hand, Marsh adds:

> Dougal Macdougal was equally far right
> and wanted, or so it was believed, to bring a
> Jacobite pretender to the throne and restore
> capital punishment.[25]

The combination of political extremes suggests that politics enlivened the working theater for Marsh. This last of the major male characters adds trouble as well as brilliance to the case. The Macbeth, Sir Dougal Macdougal, makes his entrance twenty minutes late, a star entrance, so that "Everybody felt as if the central heating had been turned up another five points.[26] All charm at first, Sir Dougal is soon in conflict with Simon and Gaston Sears.

The Duncan had played every king in Shakespeare, except for Lear and Claudius, and he looked more royal than the crowned heads he portrayed. The Malcolm is Duncan's nineteen-year-old son Seyton (played by Gaston Sears), the servant who is always at Macbeth's side, a hovering symbol for evil. He is an authority on medieval weapons with a *basso profundo* voice that rambles on interminably at any mention of the claymore, the greatsword or, as he prefers, the claidheamh-mor. Sears is less an actor than a specialist in antiquarian weapons who brandishes the claidheamh-mor ominously and teaches Macbeth and Macduff a rigorous and carefully choreographed battle scene that becomes the centerpiece not only of the play, but of the murder as well. (Among Sears' other problems is the fact that he had been previously institutionalized—and he is probably still certifiably insane.)

Lady Macduff, Nina Gaythorn, is a skilled, dependable "forty something" actress, happy to get a long run and still capable of bringing a fresh approach to her role. She is so superstitious about *Macbeth*, however, that she develops a purification ritual at home and in her dressing room and infects the others with her fanaticism.

The witches are played as entirely evil, "Dressed like fantastic parodies of Meg Merrilies but with terrible faces."[27] They are actually nice, hard-working actors though they add to the ominous nature of the production. Rangi Western, one of the witches, is a Maori whose great-grandfather was a cannibal and who teaches his fellow witches the terrifying expression of a spell-weaver. All of the actors take on the charactersistics of the roles they are playing. When they go out on the town, the cast breaks up into groups which correspond to their parts in the play.

The juvenile in this novel is a fine young lad, intelligent and committed to becoming an actor. In spite of the fact that young William and his mother are struggling financially and are doubly burdened with the stigma of having a mass murderer in the family, they make the best they can of a new life. William's unaffected personality is a pleasant surprise for the cast, as is his acting skill. He is a student at a special school for the arts, can fight, do gymnastics, and is learning karate. Emily and Peregrine Jay's boys find in him an excellent companion. In fact, their ordinary children's games help to reveal the killer's identity! Perry feels that William has the potential for success as an actor, and keeps him on in the company to play Hamnet Shakespeare in a play all his own. Although the first youngster who had played the role was an unpleasant little monster, William wins over the affection of all, including the gruff Gaston Sears, who lets him have the wooden claymore, and wishes him well in his acting career.

The stars of *Macbeth* cluster around Margaret Mannering, who has developed into one of the greatest Lady Macbeths in theatrical history. Unlike the fierce lady she plays, Margaret is one of Marsh's images of a dedicated professional actress whose fame and beauty have not affected her natural goodness. Aware that the actors who play Macbeth and Macduff are both attracted to her, she is kind to each, but declares that emotional involvement is out of the question during a production. All of her energy must go into her role, and even her dinners and private moments with her co-stars are devoted to the details of their stage performances. Although she is fond of Simon, she explains that the sexual effectiveness of her relationship with Sir Dougal is due to their acting well together. If there was to be a real life relationship, she explains, the audience would become muddled, and the impact of their acting would be destroyed: "The audience will sense there's another reality intruding on the dramatic reality and they'll feel uncomfortable."[28]

Vintage Murder depicts another play company that is the microcosm of a society in itself. The company, not surprisingly, follows most closely the closed society of the classic mystery detective novel, a form with which Marsh was most familiar. In addition, since Marsh had directed Pirandello's *Six Characters in Search of an Author*, the list of Actors of the Company may be used to summarize what to expect in the action to come: The Manager, the Leading Lady, Leading Man, Lead, L'Ingenue, Juvenile Lead, Other actors and actresses, Property Man, Prompter Machinist, Manager's Secretary, Door-Keeper, Scene-shifters. While not every person is present in each and every book, there are usually representatives of each type to be found somewhere in the novels. The lists of characters in books such as *Light Thickens*, *Night at the Vulcan*, and *Killer Dolphin* include the actors' names cross-referenced with the roles they play.

In *Vintage Murder*, as in others, the best actor of all is not *on* stage, but is a professional who works with the company's business matters. Fox's information leads to George Mason's arrest at the conclusion. Alleyn writes to his colleague:

> He got right into the skin of his part—the insignificant little dyspeptic, worrying about what would happen to the show.[29]

Alleyn is taking a trip for his health following major surgery. He is the "tall man" on a train carrying a touring company through New Zealand. Hailey Hambleton, the leading man, and actor-director of the company, noticing Alleyn's analytical gaze, asks if he finds them a queer lot. Hambleton will keep the policeman's identity a secret for him. Valerie Gaines is a rich, talentless ingenue whose father's influence got her into the company. Alleyn observes that such nepotism "seems a little unjust in an overcrowded profession."[30] But Hailey admits that it is common enough in the trade. Carolyn Dacres, the leading lady, is a great actress. She was a country parson's daughter with some stage background in her mother's family, and she has worked hard to perfect her craft.

Among the cast is Susan Max, whom Alleyn has met in *Enter a Murderer*, one of those perennial character types who has successfully adjusted to appropriate roles as she ages. She is a "real, honest-to-God actress," who had been a child performer in her grandfather's stock company, with her father as director. At the age of forty-five, she has played everything "from grande dame to trollope."[31] Susan is an example of the "useful" actor—those who can "pour themselves into the mould of a part and who did not depend upon individual tricks."[32]

Drawing on her own experiences touring New Zealand, Marsh has a good many comments to make about the drama in this novel. She speaks of

> ...that unnatural and half-ironical gaiety that
> actors often assume when greeting each other
> outside the theatre...,"[33]

of the movements which are beautiful, every gesture trained. The actors are so unconsciously professional that they seem unreal to outsiders. They begin by acting intentionally, and then their performance becomes habitual. Appearances are important to them. Actors want security, the one boon never granted them. They do not save money, often must put up a front, and they must compete with many more or at least equally talented people. As different as actors are, Alleyn seems to be one of them. Meyer tells Carolyn that Alleyn has a

> ...magnificent appearance....He'd have done
> damn well if he'd taken to "the business."[34]

In *Killer Dolphin* Marsh portrays many of the day-to-day matters of the theater. In this dream-come-true story, Peregrine "Perry" Jay accumulates a theater, writes, directs, and produces a hit play, finds an authentic Shakespearean relic, and meets the perfect woman. Although there are some problems for Perry along the way, Alleyn solves them all, since he is familiar with actors and the theater business. In the following passage Marsh explains Alleyn's connection with the stage:

Alleyn was not altogether unused to the theatrical scene or to theatrical people. He had been concerned in four police investigations in which actors had played—and "played" had been the operative word—leading roles. As a result of these cases he was sardonically regarded at the Yard as something of an expert on the species.[35]

The pleasure Peregrine and his friend Jeremy get from casting the play hypothetically is nothing compared to the thrill of working with an actual company of big name actors-even if one blackmails his way into the cast, and the juvenile is a dreadful brat. Unfortunately, both male stars are interested in the leading lady, which makes peace even more challenging for the young director.

Peregrine is blessed with a wonderful cast for his play. For Shakespeare he has Marcus Knight,

> Elizabethan Angry....Lonely. Chancy. Tricky. Bright as the sun. A Pegasus in the Hathaway stable? Enormously over-sexed and looking like the Grafton portrait."[36]

He has been Hotspur, Henry V, Mercutio, and Hamlet. He can look any age. His only drawbacks are that he is expensive and very hard to get along with. Once the whole cast quit in protest of his behavior. Once he stopped the play and told latecomers to sit down or leave. Marcus Knight is an experience unto himself:

> Marcus was an actor of whom it was impossible to say where hard thinking and technique left off and the pulsing glow that actors call star-quality began. At earlier rehearsals he would do extraordinary things: shout, lay violent emphasis on oddly selected words, make strange, almost occult gestures and embarrass his fellow players by speaking

with his eyes shut and his hands clasped in
front of his mouth as if he prayed.[37]

Perry comes to understand why the man is at the top
of his profession so young: he works hard, though eccen-
trically. The parts of Mr. W. H. and the lovely boy are
played by the same man, fair and good-looking, almost
written for W. Hartley Grove, who even has the right ini-
tials. The Dark Lady is Destiny Mead, another portrait of
the dumb actress,

> ...cement from the eyes up but she gives a
> great impression of smoldering depths and
> really inexhaustible sex. She can produce
> what's called for in any department as long
> as it's put to her in basic English and very,
> very slowly.[38]

She lives with Knight, but that does not prevent
other men from falling in love with her. Destiny looks at
Perry "with the determined adulation of some mixed-up and
sexy mediaeval saint."[39] Perry knows that she means
nothing by her looks and celebratedly sexy hoarse voice;
"She was lovely beyond compare and as simple as a
sheep."[40] But she is shrewd and does a good job once she
has had her work explained on a primary level.
    The other two actors are far more important, though
not as famous and for different reasons. Emily Dunne has
played Celia, Nerissa, and Hermia at Stratford, and been
successful on television. She is attractive and intelligent,
and becomes Perry's confidante, both in this novel and in
Light Thickens; she is content to be the helpmate of a successful director-producer. The young actor, Trevor Vere,
is an undergrown teenager whom no one likes but who
identifies the killer in a dramatic hospital scene.
    A potential victim for Marsh's murders is Gertrude
Bracey, who plays Anne Hathaway and is Grove's dis-
carded mistress and Knight's arch enemy. Like Knight she
has a peculiar approach to her role:

Gertie was enough to reduce an author-director to despair. She had after a short tour of the States become wedded to Method acting. This involved endless huddles with whoever would listen to her and a remorseless scavenging through her emotional past for fragments that could start her off on some astonishing association with her performance.[41]

Harry complains that her method is like a bargain basement. The resultant conflict creates a scene that could be typical of a disagreement within any theatrical company. She stops to think, and destroys the timing. Marcus throws a monumental temper tantrum:

Am I coupled with a harridan or a bloody dove? My author, my producer, my art tell me that here is a great moment. I should be fed, by Heaven, fed: I should be led up to....My whole being should be lacerated. And so, God knows it is, but by what!...By a driveling, piping pea-hen![42]

He rages that she should have some idea of what it is like to be scorned. Harry at that point laughs, offending both Gertie and Marcus. Gertie's reponse is to produce a virtuoso scream and tears. Marsh describes the result:

There followed a phenomenon that would have been incomprehensible to anybody who was not intimately concerned with the professional theatre. Knight and Miss Bracey were suddenly allied.[43]

From then on they act beautifully together. Although these highly tempermental performers jockey for star positions and make every attempt to upstage each other, the play goes brilliantly.

Night at the Vulcan features one of Marsh's most charming leading actresses, together with her most obnoxious playwright. She also includes a portrait of a character who may have been a great deal like the young Miss Marsh as she entered the new (to her) world of English theater. Martyne Tarne is a typical struggling actress, trudging from audition to audition with no luck and starving, literally, since her traveler's checks and letters of introduction have been stolen. But Martyne has a dream:

> Very often she had dreamed herself into a theatre where all was confusion because the leading actress had laryngitis and the understudy was useless. She would present herself modestly: "I happen to know the lines, I could perhaps..." She visualizes a hush, appreciation, wild success.[44]

Since there are no more auditions to try for and she is very tired and hungry, however, she instead presents herself as an applicant to be dresser to Helena Hamilton, who is a wonderful actress without the egotism of Mary Bellamy or La Sommita.

> She could make a curtain-speech that every leading woman in every theater in the English-speaking world had made before her and persuade the last man in the audience that it was original. She could convince bit-part actresses playing maids in first acts that there, but for the grace of God, went she.[45]

She is, however, overly generous in her affections. She goes from one passionate love affair to another, cutting off her husband, who has turned to alcohol and blackmail as emotional crutches. Alleyn admits that he does not know how to handle a *femme fatale* like her. In her pleasantly self-centered manner, she considers her love a gift and has a remarkable way of dropping a lover without regrets while considering him especially blessed because she once loved him.

But her husband nurses his pain to such an extent that it begins to affect his acting. Eventually he will become an infinitely deserving victim. He infuriates Dr. John Rutherford, the playwright, by upstaging the other actors and playing them for comedy—even tripping up one of them during a performance. He attempts to make his rather unpleasant character more sympathetic to the audience, and he has undercut the production by insisting that his niece be given the role of the ingenue, even though she is incapable of playing it.

His excessive vanity, as disgusting as it is to the rest of the company, convinces Alleyn that he could not have committed suicide. Certainly, if he were about to take his own life, he would not have bothered to touch up the makeup he hated so much. Obviously he was planning to take the curtain call for which he failed to appear.

Gay Gainsford, the hapless ingenue, is a poor actress, and even worse, she is miscast. Her awareness of her shortcomings only compounds the problem, and she is subjected to continuing insults from Rutherford, who complains that any "actress worth her salt'd memorized [her part] in an hour."[46]

He is right—and that fact enables Martyne to finally make her dream come true. When opening night jitters take their toll, Gay falls completely apart and her understudy takes over. But prior to this she has begged, and even threatened Martyne to leave the production before she is driven too far. When Jacques rescues Martyne from a particularly unpleasant scene, he notes that Gay's routine was

> ...a facade of stock emotionalism....It is a case of mis-casting....She should be in Hollywood. She has what it takes in Hollywood. What an exit! We have misjudged her.[47]

In fact Gay does her best acting off stage, particularly after her uncle's death. Upon learning that Alleyn had investigated exactly such an incident before, she intones: *"And last time it was Murder."*[48] When she tries to escape questioning, Helena Hamilton reprimands her with a brief lesson on acting: "You're not choking: if you were your eyes would water and you'd probably dribble."[49]

Alleyn dislikes her from their first meeting—she is too chameleon-like to suit his taste. She speaks

> ...in a high grand voice that seemed to come out of a drawing room comedy of the twenties.[50]

And Alleyn wonders if

> ...she had decided that her first reading of her new role was mistaken. "She's abandoned the brave little woman for the suffering mondaine who goes down with an epigram."[51]

She is untrustworthy and impersonates others by taking refuge in the characters she has played in repertory theater from such plays as *The Second Mrs. Tanquery*, *Private Lives*, and *Sleeping Partners*.

Jacques Doré, "Jocko," is a "dogsbody"; he assists the director, Adam Poole, designs sets, creates costumes, and does whatever he can to help out. He, too, plays a role:

> I have not the talent to make a character of myself for the people who sit in front, so instead I play to actors. A wheel within wheels. For twenty years I have built up my role of confidant, and now if I wanted to I couldn't leave off. For example, I can speak perfect English, but my accent is a feature of the role of Papa Jacko and must be sustained. Everybody knows it is a game and,

amiably, everyone pretends with me. It is
all rather ham and jejune, but I hope that you
are going to play too.[52]

Martyne is already "playing" to the actors in her
role as a dresser without personal ambitions, and hiding her
secrets. Jacques senses her potential from the first, and understands how much like him she really is. He becomes
her defender and supporter.

Alleyn himself plays a different sort of a role in this
novel. He serves as a mentor and teacher to Michael Lamprey and his colleagues. But he is uncharacteristically unsure that he is doing the right thing, since he has no solid
evidence. He sympathizes with the killer enough to allow
him to escape the consequences of his actions by committing suicide.

Many other actors and actresses play minor parts in
Marsh's novels. In *Singing in the Shrouds* the TV star
Aubyn Dale is handsome, vain, smooth-tongued, and an alcoholic. He fills Alleyn "together with eighty per cent of
his male viewers, with a vague desire to kick him."[53]

In *Spinsters in Jeopardy* Annabella Wells is, "a no-
toriously erratic if brilliant actress"[54] working on a French
film. She recognizes Alleyn from a trip both had taken
across the Atlantic during which she had tried to lure him
into a shipboard romance. She has kept track of him over
the years by indulging in her hobby of attending criminal
trials. Although she is a drug addict, she does not betray
him to the other cult members. Alleyn mourns her:

In the English theatre her brilliance had
been dimmed by her outrageous eccentricities, but in Paris, particularly the motion-
picture studios, she was still one of the great
ones.[55]

She is still beautiful, though ravaged by drug abuse.
Alleyn, though he is violently opposed to the use of drugs,
tries to reason with her. Reminding her of her brilliant performance as Hedda Gabler at the Unicorn in 1942, he

challenges her to prove she is still capable of that level of acting. She evades him, declaring that her latest film was the best she has ever done, and further she is still performing as well as ever. Besides, "the studio is less exacting than the theater. Will the cameras wait when the gallery would boo? I couldn't know less about it."[56]

Alleyn honestly seeks Annabella's reform, and proves it when the arrests come at the end of the novel. She slaps him, however, still unsure of his motives. When she asks if he is trying to seduce her, Alleyn responds:

> You should stick to classical drama, Shakespeare's women wouldn't fall for the insult-and-angry-seduction   stuff....Sorry. I'm forgetting Richard III.

She reminds him he has also forgotten about Beatrice and Benedick and Petruchio and Katharina. He says he meant to exclude comedy and she counters:

> How right you were. There's nothing very funny about my situation.[57]

Although Annabella does indeed represent the plight of many a performer whose skill has been squandered through drug or alcohol abuse, this whole didactic episode seems designed to showcase Marsh's anti-drug message, rather than to move along the plot of the mystery.

Death of a Peer also features an actress on the periphery of the plot who seems more designed to represent a stereotype of an unpromising professional, than to play a member of the circle in which the murder has taken place. Frid Lamprey is an aspiring actress who makes it clear that she would be a director's nightmare. She is so egocentric that Alleyn does not even bother to interview her, knowing she would make a useless witness—she is another Gay Gainsford. Alleyn has become familiar with the peculiarities of such self-centered actors early in his career.

In other novels, actors are people who just happen to become involved in the mystery. Dinah Copeland, in *Overture to Death*, has

> ...finished her dramatic course, and had managed to get into the tail end of a small repertory company where she remained for six weeks. The small repertory company then fell to pieces and Dinah returned home, an actress.[58]

Jocelyn Jerningham does not want his son marrying Dinah because she is a poor vicar's daughter and the family is in need of money. Such are her major problems. Her minor, and more humorous, problems involve her dealings with amateur actors (a situation which must have been familiar to Marsh). She demonstrates her professionalism by warning: "Don't quote Macbeth. It couldn't be more unlucky."[59]

Worse than bad luck, however, is a cast who will not learn their lines, and who insist on rattling off the lines they *do* know without inflexion, making faces, showing off, laughing, etc. Professional actors do not look at or react to each other, nor do they show off, encourage each other's antics, and insist on learning their lines from the prompter. From the play selection to the final performance, Dinah's cast is a comedy of all the things that can go wrong in an amateur company. Adding insult to injury, Miss Prentice grumbles:

> I am old-fashioned enough to think that the stage is not a very nice profession for a gentlewoman, Henry. But of course Dinah must act in our little piece. If she isn't too grand for such humble efforts.[60]

Actually, Dinah *is* on her way to success. In *Death and the Dancing Footman*, in which Troy and Alleyn stay with the Copelands, Marsh informs her readers that Dinah has become a successful professional actress.

A Wreath for Rivera portrays a peer who is "dire" but "improving" as a drummer. Although Lord Pastern plays at many roles, particuarly that of the rich eccentric, his finest performance is in hiding the fact that he is a columnist who gives advice to the lovelorn. He manages to keep his secret from everyone in the family—except the one who is his colleague on the magazine's staff. The professional actor in this case is society bandleader, Breezy Bellairs, whose

> ...expression of geniality had become habit-
> ual. He might have been a cleverly made
> ventriloquist's doll with a pale rubber face
> that was constantly and arbitrarily creased in
> a roguish grimace. His expressionless eyes
> with their large pale irises and enormous
> pupils might have been painted....Thus, hour
> after hour, he smiled at the couples who
> danced slowly past his stand; smiled and
> bowed and beat the air and undulated and
> smiled...."Hi-dee-ho-de-oh!" Mr. Bellairs
> would moan. "Gloomp-gloomp, giddy-iddy,
> hody-or-do." For this and for the way he
> smiled and conducted his band he was paid
> three hundred pounds a week by the man-
> agement of the Metronome....61

His men are paid for their musical talent and their sex appeal, not to mention their ability to endure an evening of creating what is euphemistically called "The Breezy Bellairs sound," a "hideous and extremely difficult rumpus.62 The pressure and stress of putting on such an act every evening has made Bellairs, like Annabella, a drug addict, a common problem with performers.

Camilla Campion is an innocent young actress who loses her grandfather while gaining a lover in *Death of a Fool*. Like Dinah, she does not have the community back-ing or family support she needs to make a success of her career. Her elocution lessons, however, provide the clue which unravels the mystery of who killed her grandfather during the "Dance of the Five Sons," and when, and how. "Nine-men's morris is filled up with mud," she orates, imitating her speechcraft instructor at the West London School of Drama.[63]

Her grandfather, William Andersen, is not pleased to be scolded for acting like an overplayed heavy and demands to know what kind of talk that is. When she answers that it is theatrical slang, he howls, "Don't tell me you're shaming your sex by taking up with that trash. That's the devil's counting-house, that is."[64] Because of her theatrical studies, Camilla is excited about the folk drama she finds right at home. She is polite and sensible enough, however, not to remind her grandfather that he is very much a part of the dramatic world himself.

Camilla not only shares Alleyn's ability to see people as a critic might, but she also demonstrates how an actress might react to interrogation. She sits, "like a good drama student...beautifully without looking at the chair. 'If I could pretend this was a mood-and-movement exercise,' she thought, 'I'd go into it with a good deal more poise.'" Her professional eye invests Alleyn with star quality, and she speaks as if she is evaluating a show rather than reporting a murder:

Begg does get pretty well into the skin of that character.[65]

And:

Ralph's got a rather nice sense of comedy, actually. He quite stole the show.[66]

Like Troy she sees details from an artist's point of view. Having viewed the production as theater, she remembers more than the ordinary person would.

For a skeptical moment Alleyn wonders if Camilla had "already learnt at her drama school to express the maximum of any given emotion at any time."[67] But he accepts the fact that she cannot blush and turn pale at will and was genuninely frightened. After Ralph finally has stormed in to protect her, she walks beautifully to the door to exit, and Alleyn teases, "Run along and render love's awakening. Or don't you have that one at your drama school?" How does he know she's in drama school?, she asks. "Star-quality, or something," he responds.68 He continues to tease her about her acting, and is amused by her diction practice in the night. Alleyn looks up

> ...to where a lighted and partially opened window glowed theatrically beyond a light drift of falling snow. Through the opening came a young voice. It declaimed with extraordinary detachment and great attention to consonants: *"Nine men's morris is filled up with mud."*69

Later she is heard declaiming, "Bibby bobby bounced a ball against the wall."70 All of this leads Alleyn to say, upon learning how everything fits together: "Ernie is a thistle whiffler and he whiffles thistles with a thistle whiffler. Diction exercise for Camilla Campion."71

The actors of *Grave Mistake* have missed their calling. The professional theatrical person in the book suspects two people—one from the very beginning, and another proves his lack of truthfulness when Alleyn investigates the past. Verity Preston recognizes an act when she sees one. She had worked in play production up to the age of forty-five when her father's death left her enough money to live in the family estate and write successful plays. Work in the theater has helped her overcome her basic shyness, but she remains aloof. When Alleyn wins her confidence he finds her shrewd knowledge of human nature of great value in understanding two criminals who take dramatic roles to accomplish their purposes.

The first actor is Bruce Gardener whose Scots dialect is laid on with a trowel, though he is a fine gardener. Verity tells Alleyn that the man is "a resurrection from the more dubious pages of J. M. Barrie."72 When Alleyn announces that he has discovered that Bruce is the "Corp" who served the late Mr. Carter, the actor puts on a grand act of being amazed that Claude is his officer's son. Gardener cannot believe that such a handsome fellow had produced such a "pair, sickly, ill-put-taegither apology for a man."[73] The analytical Alleyn observes:

> Flabbergasted is the word that springs to mind. From there he passed quickly to the "What a coincidence" bit and then into the realms of misty Scottish sentiment on "who would have thought it" and "had I but known" lines.[74]

Alleyn concludes

> ...that Gardener had developed a persona: probably from his boyhood, he's developed the *persona* that served him best: the honest, downright chap; winning, plausible, a bit of a character with the added slightly phoney touch of the pawky Scot. By and large...a loss to the Stage. I can see him stealing the show in superior soap.[75]

The second starring role in *Grave Mistake* is that of the society doctor, played by Dr. Basil Schramm of the expensive Greengages. When he was Basil Smythe, a struggling medical student, he and Verity had had a romance which ended with a forged check and hard feelings. He graciously admits to their acquaintance but lacks genuineness: "It seemed to Verity that he spoke in phrases that followed each other with the ease of frequent usage."[76] Investigations prove that the real Schramm had been dead a long time and that Basil probably never completed his medical studies. At the end of the novel the supposed doctor, successful and fake as ever, is off to America with the victim's fortune.

The image of society doctor as criminal also appears in *Death in a White Tie*. Alleyn is quick to recognize a carefully done pose. Dr. Davidson's office is as theatrical as a stage set, "A beautiful and expensive room, crying in devious tones of the gratitude of wealthy patients."[77] He is a thorough actor, a *poseur* who seems "so frankly theatrical and so theatrically frank."[78] He has a trick of opening his eyes that Alleyn assumes he uses on his patients.

Davidson admits that "I have a taste for the theatrical," and recalls what he saw on the night of Sir Robert Gospell's death as if "we watched it take place behind the footlights."[79] Alleyn observes critically that he presents a vivid scene. In florid prose Davidson remarks that "one expects Millament herself to come down the steps."[80] He handles direct questions about the murder smoothly, and even warns Alleyn not to draw too much upon his nervous energy as he works to solve his friend's murder. Dr. Davidson has succeeded better than one of his patients, Mrs. Halcut-Hackett, a gorgeous ex-actress from America, who has married well, and who has taken on the role of a Restoration comedy "run-around" wife.

In *Tied Up in Tinsel* the Alleyns meet some more interesting amateur actors. One of them carefully maintains a cockney accent and lower class behavior patterns in order to emphasize his humble beginnings. Another is a kindly old gent who plays the role of a Druid in an annual Christmas pageant. He is dressed in a golden outfit, complete with a beard "that wouldn't disgrace King Lear."[81] At the part at which Colonel F. Fleaton Forrester is to perform, the participants suffer from typical first night jitters, in spite of the carefully prepared, nearly professional performance.

The major role has been reserved for the stunning Cressida Tottenham. She is "in the Theatre," reports her fiancé, Hillary Bill-Tasman, having been first at some sort of academy. She is now into "Organic Expression," which is explained to Troy in one of Marsh's tongue-in-cheek send-ups of method acting:

> An O-Exposure is one thing for each of us and another for each of the *audience*. One simply hopes there will be a spontaneous emotional release....Zell—our director—well *not* a director in the establish-

> ment sense—he is our *source*—he puts enor-
> mous stress on spontaneity....At first I just
> moved about getting myself released and
> then Zell felt I ought to develop the yin-yang
> bit, if that's what it's called. You know, the
> male-female bit. So I did. I wore a kind of
> net trouser-token on my leg and I had long
> green crepe-hair pieces stuck on my left jaw.
> I must say I hated the spirit-gum. You
> know, on your skin? But it had an erotic-
> seaweed connotation that seemed to commu-
> nicate rather successfully. [82]

Troy can't help but wonder what else, if anything, Cressida
wore—and is assured that was all. Hillary suggests that,
whatever his fiancée was trying to communicate, taking off
her clothes can do nothing but please Cressida's audiences.

But Cressida has another act that proves deadly
when she learns the identity of her real father. The dream
world filled with knight's armor and the trappings of a lady
of the manor which she had constructed for herself col-
lapses, leading her into murderous realms. Although Cressida does an excellent job of shifting suspicion on to the re-
formed murderers on her fiancé's staff, she fails to get
away with her crime because her superficiality doesn't fool
Troy—and Alleyn always gets his man/woman.

Sebastian Parish, in *Death at the Bar*, becomes a
suspect because he is a bit of a rogue, even though he is a
successful actor. Parish lives high, entertaining "people
who count," maintaining memberships in expensive clubs,
and giving away money to actors down on their luck. His
resultant financial difficulties are typical of those experienced by many of the actors who appear in Marsh's works,
and subsequently draw suspicion to him when his cousin is
murdered.

The cousin, Luke Watchman, is a superb lawyer
who shares Sebastian's acting ability in his courtroom style.
Luke has always vied with Sebastian for attention, less no-
ticeably, but just as enthusiastically as his actor cousin who,
"off the stage...wooed applause with only less assiduity

than he commanded it when he faced an audience."[83]
When Luke probes for information, he hitches up his coat
lapels, a characteristic mannerism which is so dramatically
effective that Parish imitates him whenever he plays trial
scenes on stage.

Alleyn, who is himself regularly referred to as "the
Handsome Sleuth" and "the Gorgeous Brute," is struck by
the fact that Sebastian is

> ...nearly as striking off the stage as on it.[84]
> The hair on his head, a darker golden brown,
> was ruffled, for all the world as if his dresser
> had darted after him into the wings, and run
> a practiced hand through his locks.[85]

With his stage training he makes a good witness because he
can see the murder as a scene on stage.

> At first nobody touches Luke. His face
> is very white and he looks as if he'll faint.
> I'm standing near his head. Legge's still out
> in front of the dart board. He's saying
> something about being sorry. I've got it
> now. It's strange, but thinking of it like this
> brings it back to me. You, Norman, and
> Decima are at the bar. Wait a moment.
> Miss Darragh is further away near the in-
> glenook, and is sitting down.[86]

His description is vivid and helpful, particularly
when he reports that there was a great deal of movement
when the lights went out. Sebastian is a good portrait of
the really handsome, self-centered star. In spite of his
attractiveness, however, the beautiful lady for whom he and
his cousin had been rivals comes to love his artist friend.
He is also outperformed by the killer who has taken on a
new identity and appearance to hide his prison record and
does a wonderful drunk scene that convinces most people of
his innocence even though he is the obvious killer.

The list of actors involved in Marsh's mystery novels is a long one, including professionals and amateurs. As in real life, people always play roles or are mistaken for something they are not. Thus Markins in *Died in the Wool* is branded as a German spy though he is in reality a British agent, while apparently nice Douglas Grace is the fanatical German youth working as a British inventor. In *Clutch of Constables*, almost everyone has an assumed identity. In *Last Ditch* two established gentlemen, a French homemaker, and a small boy are important links in an international drug ring, though they at first appear almost stereotypically true to form. The society caterer *par excellence* of *Death in a White Tie* turns out to be a common blackmailer.

It is not surprising that Marsh uses so many actors in her novels in view of the fact that she has written that all authors write about people they have known. Certainly the number of actors is disproportionate to other professionals in her mysteries. But they are believable people who lead normal lives of rehearsals and business, not at all the fairytale creatures many people associate with a glamorous profession. In addition to being types well known to Marsh, actors help her thematically and structurally. When Alleyn is working with actors he has a greater challenge: Is it an act? Is this person hiding secrets? Actors are accustomed to portraying people's moods, as one of Marsh's most intelligent theatrical people, Perry Jay, tells the young actress Emily Dunne.

> It is our raw material. Murder. Violence. Theft. Sexual greed. They're commonplace to us. We do our Stanislavsky over them. We search out motives and associate experiences. We try to think our way into Macbeth or Othello or a witchhunt or an Inquisitor or a killer-doctor at Auschwitz and sometimes we think we've succeeded. But confront us with the thing itself? It's as if a tractor had rolled over us. *We're* nothing.[87]

Alleyn has learned to recognize the difference between an act and reality. In *A Wreath for Rivera* Alleyn explains how he knows that Carlisle Wayne has lied to him. He sounds very much like a director:

> Your hands behaved with violence and yet they trembled. After you had spoken they continued to have a sort of independent life of their own. Your left hand kneaded the gloves and your right hand moved rather aimlessly across your neck and over your face. You blushed deeply and stared very fixedly at the top of my head. You presented me, in fact, with Example A from any handbook on behavior of the lying witness. You were a glowing demonstration of the bad liar.[88]

In *Night at the Vulcan* Helena Hamilton, an experienced actress who knows all the tricks of the trade, realizes that her inexperienced niece is only pretending to have a physical ailment, and instructs her in the art of "suffering" convincingly. Dealing with people who are as familiar with the tell-tale signs of fear and prevarication as he is presents Alleyn with great challenges. On the positive side, his theatrical "suspects" may choose to use their training and knowledge to assist him, as Verity Preston does, in sniffing out when one of the others is putting on an act.

Alleyn obviously enjoys working with these actors—even though they tend to complicate matters. They are technicians of emotion who wear their hearts on their sleeves, rather than suppress their feelings. Marsh's relatively bloodless murders owe a good deal of their appeal to their theatrical settings. Detective and suspects alike all play roles, and the reader who wants to maintain a grip on reality, must view these tales with the same careful objectivity displayed by the protagonists, Alleyn, Fox and Troy.

APPENDIX I

ACTORS AND OTHERS ASSOCIATED WITH THE THEATRE WHO ARE KILLERS IN MARSH'S FICTION

Harry Grove, in *Killer Dolphin*
Felix Gardener, in *Enter a Murderer*
Gaston Sears, in *Light Thickens*
Cressida Tottenham, in *Tied Up in Tinsel*
Breezy Bellairs, in *A Wreath for Rivera*
Robert Legge, in *Death at the Bar*
Simon Begg, in *Death of a Fool*
Bruce Gardener, in *Grave Mistake*
Eleanor Prentice, in *Overture to Death*
Montague Reece, in *Photo Finish*
Douglas Grace, in *Died in the Wool*
Charles Templeton, in *False Scent*
Dr. Rutherford, in *Night at the Vulcan*
George Mason, in *Vintage Murder*

ACTORS AND OTHERS ASSOCIATED WITH THE THEATER WHO ARE VICTIMS IN MARSH'S FICTION

Mary Bellamy, in *False Scent*
Sir Dougal Macdougal, in *Light Thickens*
Isabella Sommita, in *Photo Finish*
Arthur Surbonadier, in *Enter a Murderer*
Clark Bennington, in *Night at the Vulcan*
Carlos Rivera, in *A Wreath for Rivera*
Sir Henry Ancred, in *Final Curtain*
William Andersen, in *Death of a Fool*
Idris Campanula, in *Overture to Death*
Jobbins, in *Killer Dolphin*
Props, in *Enter a Murderer*
Alfred Meyer, in *Vintage Murder*

IV.

AS YOU LIKE IT

MARSH AND THE SHAKESPEAREAN INFLUENCE

The use of Shakespearean names, references, quotations, themes, and plots is something that evolved into a trademark of the Alleyn detective stories after *A Man Lay Dead*. Marsh's first novel made use of then-current literary conventions by mimicking the ever-popular Agatha Christie and Dorothy Sayers books. More importantly, its publication gave Ngaio Marsh needed exposure and won her an appreciative audience. After her initial taste of success, however, she felt free to create a unique style utilizing materials gleaned from her career as a Shakespearean producer and director. Thus Alleyn views his world in the same way his creator does—and Marsh writes about what she knows best—her beloved theater.

Even upon the most elementary level, the use of Shakespearean "names" in the works is notable. Although some names are so common that her choice may have had nothing at all to do with Shakespeare, others are too unusual to be coincidental (i.e., *Oberon*). In addition there is "Caley Bard" of *Clutch of Constables* and "Mr. Baradi" in *Spinsters in Jeopardy*, whose names would seem to be plays on the Bard's occupation. A few names from the plays might be deemed coincidental; the many characters with Shakespearean "ties" listed in Appendix III, however, would suggest a design. Sir Henry Ancred (of *Final Curtain*) names most of his children after characters in his previous stage triumphs (*The Lady of Lyons*, *Othello* and *The Bells*).

71

Indeed his only "sensible" son is called Thomas, a reflection of the fact that Henry was not involved in a play at the time of his birth. Marsh has borrowed names from other playwrights as well. Mr. Pace (the travel agent in *When in Rome*) shares his name with a comic Italian, Mrs. Pace, who appears in *Six Characters in Search of an Author*. Many of Marsh's characters refer to the Bard, but only two, Bruce Barrabell, a vindictive trouble-maker and Mr. Merryman, a psychopathic killer, speak ill of him.

Shakespeare's use of pairs to contrast the lower against the upper classes has been appropriated by Marsh as well. Alleyn and Fox (as mentioned in Chapter II) are deliberately paired off with their equivalents in many of the cases. Alleyn is summoned formally by Lady Carterette in *Scales of Justice* and by Mr. Conducis in *Killer Dolphin*, and he is strongly "requested" by Montague Reece in *Photo Finish*. In contrast, Fox is the man who is sent by the CID to begin bringing order to the crime scene. Alleyn frequently conducts his interviews on stage, or in the library, while Fox heads to the kitchen to question the servants. Alleyn speaks like an Oxford professor—Fox's language is that of the local pub, peppered with colloquialisms and earthy *bon mots*. Although Fox rarely uses quotes, Alleyn sprinkles his conversation liberally with quotations, particularly when he is dealing with actors. Had Marsh followed Shakespeare's example more faithfully, Alleyn would speak verse, while Fox spoke prose.

Alleyn's suspects are frequently well-educated, famous, wealthy and/or of the aristocracy. But Marsh includes some wonderful common folk to enliven things. Fred Badger is a night watchman at the Vulcan Theatre who takes pity on the starving Martyne Tarne. He is effusive, simple, good-hearted, and more than willing to share his food and find a place where the exhausted girl can sleep safely. When he hears Martyne might be implicated in the case, he goes straight to Alleyn to report that Martyne was "safe in the arms of Morpus"[1]—wording worthy of Dogberry.

In Shakespearean plays such as *Julius Caesar* or *Coriolanus* there are scenes in which common people are allowed to comment on the major character thus setting the scene as viewed by the everyday world. In *Death of a Peer* a knife-grinder is told by a newsboy that "Endsome Elleen" (Alleyn) is up at Pleasaunce Court, along with the camera man and fingerprint expert. A fatal accident has taken place, and the Yard has been called in to investigate. Marsh was apparently dissatisfied with this device, and did not use the technique for exposition again, although in *Light Thickens* she comes close to it. The cast goes in to a bar for drinks after rehearsal, and the barman becomes involved in a discussion with the actors about their various eccentricities and superstitions, in particular their avoidance of the very mention of the work they are rehearsing.

Shakespeare often used young boys in his plays, and school-age youngsters frequently became affiliated with the acting companies on a temporary basis. Boys stood in for women in Shakespeare's time, and especially talented lads shone as the sons of Macduff or Coriolanus, models of precocious children who can see reality without preconception. The child actor is still a theater staple, and Marsh has used them to advantage in such works as *Killer Dolphin*, *Light Thickens*, and, briefly, in *Death of a Fool*. In *Overture to Death* a child's prank inspires the murderer to booby-trap the piano her victim is to play with a real gun rather than a toy. In *Death of a Peer* eleven-year-old Michael Lamprey gets his first taste of criminal investigation and wins Alleyn's affection. Little Sissy Stimson has to be bribed and entertained by Alleyn and Angela to persuade her to provide needed information in *A Man Lay Dead*. Alleyn has the ability to charm the truth from the youngsters in these cases.

Trevor Vere of *Killer Dolphin* is an eleven-year-old, an actor, and a repulsive egotist who is the only person who can identify the murderer correctly. Although he comes close to being a victim himself, Trevor manages to escape with a broken thigh and ribs, a cut on the head, and a bruised jaw. He spends time in the hospital receiving visitors and reading comic books. William Smith, the boy in *Light Thickens*, is attending a special school for the arts where he is receiving a superior education. Together with

Peregrine Jay's boys, he identifies the killer. Though the lads know who is responsible for the deaths they are never in danger. Marsh allows her young actors a special grace, and shields them from harm.

In *Dead Water* Wally Trehern is a young boy who is exploited for the tourist business on Portcarrow Island. Wally apparently undergoes a miraculous cure at the local spring through the offices of a beautiful "Green Lady." Wally is very much like the Shakespearean fool, and is incapable of lying. Although he reflects the village's hostility toward Miss Pride, he understands that Miss Cost is not as good-hearted as she would like everyone to believe. Alleyn knows that the boy's intelligence is limited, but he is aware of what is taking place around him. He parrots the "line" promoting Pixie Falls, but at the same time he is able to see and report helpful clues. His final utterance, "All gone," is a *double entendre*, indicating that not only are his warts all gone, but that the mysteries of the Green Lady and the murder are over as well.

Ricky Alleyn, the only child of sensitive and intelligent parents, combines his mother's artistic skills with his father's ability to sort out a crime scene. He is referred to in several of the Alleyn books, appearing as a precocious child in *Spinsters in Jeopardy*, and as an aspiring novelist in *Last Ditch*. He is described as charming and as vulnerable as the children in *Richard III*.

Both Troy and Alleyn are doting parents who play with their son while treating him as a small adult. Alleyn, the dignified inspector, chants "How many miles to Babylon," as he sits the small boy on his shoulders. Contemplating his son, he thinks: "Ricky had the newly made look peculiar to little boys in bed."[2] Ricky is terrified at being separated from his parents, "dithering with agitation" when parted from them for a few minutes."[3] In the midst of his excitement, however, Ricky falls asleep, a normal small boy.

Ricky wins friends easily. Raoul Milano, the Alleyn's driver, buys him a little silver grey goat mounted on a base in the shape of a chateau. Ricky loves the goat, charmed by the way it lights up in the dark. Troy goes into hysterics when she returns to their hotel to find him gone. He has indeed been kidnapped, but fortunately one of his captors is Raoul's beautiful but stupid sweetheart. Ricky, who is fairly fluent in French, keeps asking her "*Pourquois*?" Alleyn traces him to a chemical factory rather easily, though Ricky sobs, "Another time you'd jolly well better be a bit quicker!"4

Ricky is able to identify his captors, and soon his fright is forgotten and he falls fast asleep—but not before he has revealed to his parents that P. E. Garbel is a woman, providing Alleyn with the insights he needs to break a satanic cult and the drug ring of which it is part. Ricky is more than just a charming little appendage to his illustrious father. Certainly his presence in the novel has the added advantage of making Alleyn seem just a bit more human than usual.

Alleyn takes the children in his cases seriously, often learning crucial pieces of information from them which help him to identify the killer. Marsh viewed children characters as "small people," who should be treated with respect. A child has a certain kind of perceptiveness which can be likened to that of a good policeman. A child on stage can also provide a very effective visual contrast to the other actors, and is a sure audience winner.

Though they refer more often to the tragedies, the mysteries of Ngaio Marsh have a great deal more in common with Shakespeare's comedies. Roland Mushat Frye, in *Shakespeare, the Art of the Dramatist*, has used the phrase, "The green world and the environs of comedy" to describe the frequency with which Shakespearean characters escape from the everyday world (especially from the city) into a fresher environment, where fewer people imply fewer complications to a working-through of their problems. The Bard's Forest of Arden may be compared to the remote game lodge, where Marsh's closed society of the formal detective novel holds forth. Marsh, in fact, has created some unique, off-the-beaten-path settings for her tales: estates locked in by snow; small villages; and sheep ranches in the outback, where a few select suspects can be questioned at leisure.

Other characteristics of Shakespearean comedy noted by Frye are: an atmosphere permeated with optimism; a genial, non-satiric tone; a festive ending; the predominance of young lovers and marriages; background roles for older characters; and the muting of evil. Marsh opposes fakery of all sorts, but there is a certain geniality to her writing, and she is never truly satirical in the fun she pokes at her characters. Her endings are not shoot-'em-up scenes of gratuitous violence, and even the suicides in *Died in the Wool* and *Night at the Vulcan* do not cause undue pain for others. Although her endings are not festive in the Shakespearean sense of peasants dancing, they do, in general, have happy results.

In *Hand in Glove*, Pyke Period is able to establish that he is indeed a genuine member of a proud family, even though he was omitted from the church register when an absent-minded rector forgot to write down the names of both twins. And Andrew Bantling glories in the fact that Troy Alleyn is taking him on as one of her few private pupils. Even Mary Bellamy's funeral at the end of *False Scent* is a festive occasion because it fulfills her favorite daydream. Murderers may die (as in *False Scent*) or be institutionalized for mental care (as in *Light Thickens*), but rarely do they suffer a violent death. And Alleyn, who may be said to be inspired by his creator, opposes capital punishment with a passion.

One of the main characteristics of comedy writing, beginning with the classicists of ancient Greece, has not been the so-called "happy" ending, however, but the union of lovers. Early comedy was traditionally expressed in the ritual celebration of marriage and the beginning of the couple's new life together. Marsh's novels almost always feature a romantic pair of young lovers who must overcome obstacles set up by their parents and/or social customs. Notably among these are the two novels in which Alleyn pursues Troy. The couples are usually young and bright, like Nigel and Angela, with a bit of "Beatrice and Benedick" in them. Matchmaker Marsh unites Bartholomew and the contralto, Sylvia Perry in *Photo Finish*,

Fenella and Paul in *Final Curtain*, and Richard and Anelida in *False Scent*.

Occasionally the romance is challenged because the man is older and more experienced: Peregrine and Emily in *Killer Dolphin*, Adam and Martyne in *Night at the Vulcan*, or Sophy and Barnaby in *When in Rome* are cases in point. In one example, a love story develops between the retired diplomat, Sam Whipplestone, and Lucy Lockett, a personable and shrewd kitten of a girl. Usually, the romance ends in marriage (or a settled home in the previously lonely Sam's case).

Older people often give advice to young lovers in Shakespeare's plays, and in Marsh's works, as well. Troy, Fox, and Alleyn fill supporting roles just by being good listeners to their young charges. In *Singing in the Shrouds* Alleyn helps Brigid, who has just recovered from heartbreak and does not want to be hurt again, by admitting that the great love of his life began with a shipboard romance. Troy stands by Fenella and Paul. Kind people like Octavius Browne in *False Scent* and Verity Preston in *Grave Mistake* provide good sense and mediation in time of turmoil. During the courting of Troy, Alleyn's perceptive mother acts as counsel to both her son and the woman she would like to have as a daughter-in-law.

In Marsh's work a couple is joined as the crime is solved, and even those who have postponed their union for a long time may come together at last: Jonathan Royal and Lady Hersey Amblington, and Aubrey Mandrake and Chloris Wynne in *Death and the Dancing Footman*, for example, as well as Commander Syce (who promises to stop drinking) and Nurse Kettle in *Scales of Justice*. Robin Herrington and Ginny Taylor swear off drugs and begin planning their wedding at the end of *Spinsters in Jeopardy*. Henry Lamprey looks for a job, so he can support his prospective bride, Robin Grey, in *Death of a Peer*. When the case is over in *The Nursing Home Murder*, Angela expresses hope that Sir John Phillips and Nurse Jane Harden can finally marry to satisfy her craving for a happy ending. Alleyn reports: "We don't often see it in the force."[5]

Marsh, however, usually gives the survivors of Alleyn's cases cause for celebration.

During Shakespeare's heyday Ben Jonson and other critics often were unsettled by the popular dramatist's defiance of the so-called Aristotelian unities. The drunken Porter featured in *Macbeth* or Beatrice's dramatic call to "Kill Claudio" in *Much Ado About Nothing* bothered them. Hamlet clowns; Iago jokes; parents threaten to kill their daughters, or relegate them to convents. Shakespeare seemes to be confusing comedy and tragedy indiscriminately.

From the time of Poe and Doyle, however, the mystery genre has often combined satiric overtones with humorous characters and dialogue—in spite of the grimness and death depicted therein. The American hard-boiled P.I. novel, for example, is well-renowned for leaving a slightly gritty aftertaste, no matter how successful the detective might be in solving the case at hand against all odds. Marsh, then, is not unique in her blending of comic and tragic elements.

Alleyn may occasionally empathize with the killer, even when he is a psychopathic mass murderer, as in *Singing in the Shrouds*. Marsh's most evil villain of all, the Jampot in *Clutch of Constables*, is treated with a certain grudging admiration for his technical skill. Murderers can be driven to their dastardly deeds by jealousy, anger, or even a need to protect a loved one. In many of these cases of "love gone wrong," the perpetrator may be incarcerated and treated as someone who is ill, rather than as a monster. The monsters of the real world, in fact, do not appear on the pages of Ngaio Marsh's novels. She prefers to solve the problems of her literary world in a more genial fashion.

Not to say there are no ugly death scenes in Marsh's works. Mention could be made of: the poisoning of Garcia, in *Artists in Crime*; the skewer through the eye of Gabriel, Marquis of Wutherwood and Rune, in *Death of a Peer*; or the beheading of Dougal Macdougal in *Light Thickens*. There is, however, no sense of really nasty corruption in Marsh, who is not a great believer in evil. Compared to their counterparts in real life, the drug dealers are pussycats—a little like Shakespeare's Don John: ugly, distasteful, even a little comic—but never threatening to the hero. The beating of Ricky by Ferrant and Jones, in *Last Ditch*, is the worst thing that happens to the young man. The bad guys are too stupid to notice the "P.A.D." signature on the note sent to Alleyn, an obvious indication of Ricky's whereabouts.

Marsh shares another trait with Shakespeare—the strength of their women characters. Marsh usually features at least two strong women characters in each mystery, as Shakespeare did in his comedies. Dramatically, the leading lady and the ingenue provide a contrast, hard work and talent, perhaps, vs. beauty and financial influence—as in *Vintage Murder* and *Killer Dolphin*. They may also vary in their sizes and coloring, as do Martyne and Helena, one short and dark, the other fair and tall, a technique which is visually effective on stage.

Marsh's women are not the legendary "dames" of the American hard-boiled detective stories. Brigid O'Shaunnessy (in the *Maltese Falcon*) was an expert criminal. Marsh, instead, features someone like Flossie Rubrick, a Member of Parliament and a powerful sheep ranch supervisor. She is a performer, too, a great orator who died, ironically, while practicing a forty-five minute speech in a woodshed. After all his interviews, Alleyn believes he understands her well enough to regret he never really knew her when she was alive.

Other women, like Dame Alice Mardian, in *Death of a Fool*, are eccentric matriarchs or, like Miss Emily Pride, order Alleyn and Fox around through the sheer force of their personalities. Actresses are important in the theater, and here they naturally play roles larger than life as well. Marsh includes a wide range of females in her repertoire, ranging from killer to victim, from quiet homemaker and policeman's wife (Mrs. Plank, in *Last Ditch*) to millionaire art collector (Mrs. Guzmann in *Killer Dolphin*).

Troy is the model woman in Marsh's novels. She is loving, yet independent. Her Shakespearean parallel is Portia, of *The Merchant of Venice*, notable for her innate intelligence and ability to understand people. In *Tied Up in*

Tinsel and *Spinsters in Jeopardy* she and Alleyn carry on a Prospero-and-Miranda-like routine. Alleyn voices his violent antipathy to the drug trade, which he feels, aside from war, is the worst thing that has happened in his time. He softens his tirade with Shakespearean bantering, and dialogue borrowed from *The Tempest*:

> "Dost thou attend me?" Alleyn asks.
> "Sir, most heedfully," Troy responds.

Later he checks:

> "Thou attendest not."
> "Oh, good sir, I do," protests Troy.
> "I pray thee, mark me."

Marsh notes: "They exchanged the complacent glance of persons who recognize each other's quotations."[6]

When Alleyn first confesses his love for her (in *Artists in Crime*), Troy remains hesitant about accepting his declaration, and Alleyn is as distraught as any Elizabethan sonneteer. In a rather undignified moment he even makes a face at Troy's current gentleman friend's picture—then feels foolish. But after she is willing to listen to him, his gloom turns to silliness, and he drives so fast that Fox suspects something is happening to his partner. A talk with Miss Troy, Fox observes, always cheers up Alleyn.

At the end of the novel there is an idyllic tryst in a rose garden. (The scene is reminiscent of Portia and Bassanio at Belmont.) Alleyn summarizes the case, and establishes Troy as his most receptive non-Yard confidante. He stops being his competent self and becomes sentimental, in a scene that has very little to do with the case he has just solved. Troy confesses that, in spite of her fear of physical and emotional involvement, she loves him too. It is a daydream come true for such a woman. Her man has pleaded for her, and has allowed her to set her own terms. The resultant marriage between these two is one of equals, with mutual respect and the right to be alone to develop their separate, successful lives.

Troy is not the only woman to have a bargaining position in a love affair with a highly desirable man other women could not hold. Peregrine Jay has just broken off a dead-end relationship with an actress when Emily Dunne enters his life with her talent and intelligence. Apparently his former love was as emptyheaded as Destiny Mead while Emily can discuss Shakespeare or philosophize on his level. Emily is a good person, virtuous, loyal, and not about to use her charms to catch the bright young producer-director-playwright. But she does, and holds him, as we learn in *Light Thickens*, when she is as much his support and confidante as Troy is Alleyn's.

Another case of a woman who hesitates to accept a man who can free her from suspicion of murder comes in *Night at the Vulcan*, when Martyne Tarne finds that a man who is her director, distant relative, and supporter loves her. A man with such fame, looks, and influence, whom she has admired in films, and who is (as Mike Lamprey cattily points out) old enough to be her father could easily be using his influence to manipulate her feelings. So Martyne holds back from this daydream romance. He assures her that he is not in the habit of making passes at young ladies in his company, and admits that he has had an affair with Helena Hamilton that has come to an end peacefully, although he says that he was honored by her love.

Their exchange of affection is stage-worthy, spoken in theatrical metaphors. Martyne begins:

> I can't help feeling this scene is being played at the wrong time, in the wrong place and before the wrong audience. And I doubt...if it should be played at all.[7]

Adam Poole continues the comparison:

> ...this scene has been played so awkwardly—inaudible, huddled up, inauspicious and uneffective. Technically not altogether bad. It gives a kind of authority, I hope.[8]

There is no pressure on Martyne whose romance is conducted in lines like those of a Shakespearean comedy. In fact, many *are* lines from Shakespeare. When Gay breaks down and cannot go on stage, Adam cheers her with "That's my girl." she quips, "...I must say...you do well to quote Petruchio. And Henry the Fifth, if it comes to that." Adam responds:

> A brace of autocratic male animals? Therefore it must follow you are "Kate" in two places. And shrewd Kate, French Kate, kind Kate, but never curst Kate.[9]

Shortly after, Helena asks why Adam calls Martyne Kate. "I suspect her...of being a shrew," he cheerfully responds.[10] In reality, Martyne is adversary and lover, protecting Gay from being fired from her role and being too proud to accept attention that she feels is pity. After a short time, the main scenes between Martyne and Adam are wooing.

Another woman who has things her way is Camilla Campion in *Death of a Fool*. She loves Ralph Stayne who comes to her rescue when he thinks Alleyn is grilling her. But Ralph has had a well-known affair with flamboyantly sexy Trixie, the bar maid. On Alleyn's advice, Ralph tells Camilla about the affair which occurred before she came into his life. She is in a position to forgive or reject him, he leaves it up to her. In these cases and others, Marsh's women fulfill the ideal of the Wife of Bath. Women are not passive receivers of love.

Another characteristic of Shakespeare's comedies is the inclusion of a hint of real violence. In a play as light as *A Midsummer Night's Dream* there is the risk of death to the young lovers. *Twelfth Night* includes a shipwreck and a duel that would easily have ended the heroine's life. *As You Like It* finds one brother trying to kill another and a man hunt in the forest. *Much Ado About Nothing* has the ugly scene of a groom denouncing his bride in front of her family and friends. The pound of flesh demanded in the *Merchant of Venice* is truly ominous. However, just as fears for the safety of Shakespeare's comic characters never last long, Marsh's "nice" people usually survive. Only Jobbins of *Night at the Vulcan*, killed accidentally, Alfred Meyer, killed to cover financial dishonesty in *Vintage Murder*, and Lord Robert Gospell of *Death in a White Tie* (whom everyone loved and whose kindness brightened the lives of many a wallflower) are the only victims who generate sympathy.

Marsh's victim is usually the person whose demise would benefit the greatest number of people. Although the killer's motives may be weak, the victim is unpleasant enough to stir up the homicidal fantasies of numerous people, leading Alleyn to the conviction that motive is a relatively minor part of the murder case.

Character, in fact, is the greatest single factor in Alleyn's investigation. It is not *why* one person murders another which fascinates him, but *whose* personality is most likely to turn homicidal—given the right conditions. In the mystery genre, the reader often is not given enough information about the victim to feel sympathy either for or against him; in Marsh's works the reader is led to conclude, as does the murderer, that the victim is an obstacle which ought to be "removed." In many of Alleyn's cases the tragedy over the loss of a human life is overcome by the promise of a new beginning for at least one couple. The death of an individual who seriously impedes the happiness of others leaves us with a sense of wrongs righted and justice fulfilled.

Even without his magnificent characters and unforgetable language, Shakespeare's plays would stand the test of time simply because he was one of the world's greatest storytellers. Many of Shakespeare's tales can be traced back to some of the most elemental plots of all time. Just as he himself was known to borrow lines from earlier sources, modern writers have adopted his plots and motifs for such popular works as *West Side Story, Kiss Me Kate, MacBird,* and *Rosenkranz and Guildenstern Are Dead,* among many others. Rare is the person who has not identified with Hamlet's despair or recognized Falstaff in a business associate at one time or another. Marsh, no stranger to Shakespeare's genius, has used certain of the plays to enrich her own stories.

The Taming of the Shrew (as well as the love scene in *Henry V*), has already been mentioned in *Night at the Vulcan*. Martyne Tarne's desire is to be a success on her own rather than relying on Adam Poole's relationship to her family, but Martyne is no Kate in terms of personality. The unhappy, unloved character who strikes out in frustration appears instead in the form of Gay Gainsford. The comic figures are the bombastic dramatist, Dr. John Rutherford and Jacques, who cheers people up through his kindly deeds. Bianca is, of course, Helena Hamilton, the leading lady with whom everyone falls in love. She is a lovely creature, and accustomed to adulation without arrogance (unlike Mary Bellamy of *False Scent*). In the end, Alleyn observes that Jacques has long adored Helena and wonders if they will become a pair, Gay Gainsford has, in spite of her erratic behavior, won the heart of J. G. Darcy, and Martyne and Adam have come to terms. Thus, just as in *Shrew*, there are three happy couples, when the murder is solved.

Another popular Shakespearean plot device is that of the handsome Black protagonist with a strong personality. His troubling play *Othello* features a virtuous hero who is a stranger to the society in which he is expected to function. The snake Iago explains to the unwitting Othello that wives in Venice often are unfaithful and it is customary for best friends to share the same woman as wife and mistress. Othello believes Iago and resorts to solving the problem of his wife's supposed adultery with violence, as he might have in his own land. But the culture Shakespeare wrote for no longer condoned killing an adultressm, and it is murder, not justice, which occurs in the last act.

In *Black as He's Painted*, the parallel is obvious. The Boomer, Bartholomew Opala, is a brilliant lawyer. He is Alleyn's best friend from school days, a gloriously attractive subject for Troy's portrait skills and, as a Ng'ombwana leader, he is a man some 200,000 people might want dead. Opala comes to London for a state visit, mainly, the reader learns, to solve some political problems on the home front. When the Ambassador is speared at a formal reception at the Embassy, Boomer's problems are over—and Alleyn's begin.

Alleyn senses some things about his friend he cannot prove at first, although he observes that The Boomer "had changed into a dressing-gown and looked like Othello in the last act.[11] And Alleyn is horrified when Opala announces that he is happy to be rid of the odious Sanskrits. Understanding the Boomers' value system is difficult for Alleyn. He reflects on an incident from their schooldays when they went out walking and, deep in conversation, suddenly found that they had been separated by a ravine.

The Boomer asks for Alleyn's understanding:

> Justice has been done in accordance with our need, our grass-roots, our absolute selves. With time we shall evolve a change and adapt and gradually such elements may die out in us. At the present, my very dear friend, you must think of us—of me if you like—as—...—as an unfinished portrait.[12]

This statement asks that we place the concepts of right and wrong within the context of time and place. Although she was a staunch opponent of capital punishment, Marsh still respected the fact that the Maoris with whom she grew up were descendants of cannibals. They ate their victims, according to ancient beliefs, in order to absorb their enemies' powers and virtues. British concepts of right and wrong had nothing to do with the Maoris' choices or behavior. Although The Boomer was educated in British law, he chose his people's method of justice as a way of resolving his problems. The difference between Shakespeare's character and Marsh's is that Othello destroys the thing he loves by succumbing to jealousy. Opala's actions were well-founded and meant the survival of good government for his people.

Singing in the Shrouds is full of characters who talk about drama more than might be expected of average travelers. A young couple, Dr. Tim Makepiece and Brigid

Carmichael, discuss Elizabethan verse, a volume of which she happens to be reading, and Tim assumes that Shakespeare is everyone's favorite poet. Inspired by the problem of Mr. Cuddy's wandering eye, and by Aubyn Dale's ability to make men jealous of him, Tim and Brigid discuss Othello's jealousy,

While their chatting is merely pleasant speculation, Philip Merryman, a bachelor who teaches English in a small public school, lectures in the most obnoxious manner. He goes about grumbling things like "Detested kite" and "Blasts and fogs upon you!"[13] and holds that one opinion only—his—must reign.

Merryman claims that *Hamlet* is, "an inconsistent, deficient and redundant *réchauffé* of some absurd German melodrama," and *Macbeth* is, "merely a muddle-headed blunderer. Strip away the language and what remains? A tediously ignorant expression of defeatism."[14] He raves about the *Duchess of Malfi* and praises *Titus Andronicus*, *Othello*'s classical structure, and *Lear*'s last act. In reality, he is giving a clue to the identity of the psychopathic killer, who is acting out his homicidal jealousy for his stupid mother who hurt him as a child. The plays that Merryman extols include the death of a woman by some form of strangulation. He supports Othello, even after Desdemona's murder, when he propounds that "it's a tragedy of simplicity and—and greatness of heart being destroyed by a common smarty-smarty little placefinder."[15]

To make the comparison even stronger, Marsh's characters view Orson Welles' film production of *Othello*. Merryman can be heard "softly invoking the retribution of the gods on the head of Mrs. Orson Welles"[16] as he watches. Alleyn is himself "flabbergasted" by the film. The scene of Desdemona's death goes on at length; then the ship's power goes out. Protesting "this slaughterous—this impertinent travesty," Merryman storms out,[17] and almost immediately, there is another murder aboard the ship. Sexual jealousy and an unstable personality have caused four deaths by manual strangulation. After the last murder, the killer sleeps like a baby, as if, Alleyn writes to Troy, "he'd expiated a deadly crime instead of committing one."[18]   He punishes women who remind him of his mother. He and Othello have the same perverted sense of justice and the same conviction that their duty is to serve as executioners.

Perhaps one of the most common themes in love stories is the *Romeo and Juliet* story. Since Marsh pairs off lovers regularly, it is not surprising that some have family opposition.   Less acceptable than that romance was the marriage of Camilla's parents, which her grandfather, William Andersen, never approved. In *Overture to Death* the opposition is only on the basis of not enough money in the lady's family, though the fathers are friends. Disapproval is most vociferous from an aunt. Furious with Dinah for being an actress, Miss Prentice forces the young lovers to stay apart and reports whatever they do to Sir Jocelyn. Alleyn, however, smooths over the dispute at the same time he solves the murder.

More closely parallel to *Romeo and Juliet* is *Scales of Justice* which features lovers Rose Carterette and Dr. Mark Lacklander whose fathers are feuding. As much as her father loves her, Rose weeps in vain: "...*his* father says that if Mark marries me, he'll never forgive him and that they'll do a sort of a Montague and Capulet thing at us and, darling, it wouldn't be much fun for Mark and me, would it, to be star-crossed lovers?"[19] The feud ends with the death of Colonel Carterette because of his wife's affair with a younger man. But Mark and Rose are joined, as are Nurse Kettle and Commander Syce, an alcoholic who hopes to reform for his lady.

Death in a White Tie and *False Scent* both have romances that are discouraged by parents. Although Donald Potter, the profligate and selfish nephew of Lord Robert Gospell, and Bridget O'Brien seem to be sadly mismatched, Alleyn's exposure of Withers and support for the young couple makes that difference.   The nice girl, after all, knows the boy is not as much oa a cad as everyone thinks. (He is!) In *False Scent* Richard Dakers loves Analida Lee, which should be no problem since he is not only nice but a brilliant playwright who gets along well with everyone; but Mary Bellamy is insanely jealous of younger actresses and wants the young man to write only for her, even though she doesn't admit that she is his mother until she loses all control of her temper.

In *Death of a Fool* there are numerous references to *Romeo and Juliet*, including Ralph's throwing snow at Camilla's window to catch her attention and being greeted with the famous balcony scene lines. Marsh also uses the Balcony Scene in *Hand in Glove* when Lady Bantling yells up to Harold Cartell from under his window. "What light from yonder window breaks?"[20] she inquires playfully. Since Mr. Pyke Period was there too, Alleyn calls them "a brace of Romeos in reverse."[21] Ricky, similarly, is summoned by Louis Pharamond in *Last Ditch*. "But soft, what light from yonder window breaks," he says in a "stagey" voice after throwing fine gravel at Ricky's window.[22] A short love scene ensues, with Julia reciting, "Out upon you, fie upon you Bold Faced Jig," scarcely a romantic situation for the infatuated young man.[23] One thing is consistent: none of the lovers, even if family-crossed, have anything to do with murder.

Two novels are directly related to Shakespeare through repeated references and themes. *Death of a Fool* is full of references to *King Lear*. In this novel the dramatic element and the mystery are closely interwoven. The portrayal of action is made more vivid through the eyes of a wonderful stock character, Mrs. Bünz, who is a passionately dedicated Teutonic devotee of folk drama, and through those of the aspiring actress, Camilla Campion. Dr. Otterly, a country physician from a line of fiddlers, expands on the deeper meanings of the dance. He is amazed that theater folks do not scorn ritual dancing, but he is far more sympathetic to Camilla's ambitions than is her grandfather. Her ambition of playing Shakespeare pleases Otterly. In ten years, he suggests she will be playing

Not the giantesses, I fancy. Not the Lady M, nor yet the Serpent of the Old Nile. But a Viola, now, or—what do you say to a Cordelia?[24]

After playing the fiddle for thirty years, Dr. Otterly has a theory about King Lear:

> In our Five Sons is nothing more or less than a variant of the Basic Theme, Frazer's theme—the King of the Wood, the Green Man [the village pub is called the "Green Man"], the Fool, the Old Man Persecuted by His Young—the theme, by Guiser, that reached its full stupendous blossoming in *Lear.*[25]

The Dance, then, is the original of Lear.

Another folklorist's discovery supports his theory of the parallel of the dance to *Lear*. Spying on the practice, Mrs. Bünz observes what appears to be the old Guiser writing a will and showing it to the sons one after the other. She marvels at the complexity of the dance and burns with curiosity to know what the dialogue is. Her passion for knowledge drives her to get as close as she can to learn those words, even if it means buying a new cape and wearing the heavy hobby horse costume to do so. Her spying and actual participation in the dance breaks all tradition and, as Ernie believes, brings bad luck.

The conflict over succession to the starring role replaces the question of who will inherit the kingdom. Who will play the Guiser, since the old man is weakened by heart disease? Ernie, the youngest son, is a natural "fool" in the old tradition, an epileptic, an odd fellow who says whatever pops in his mind, which is always the truth, though slightly veiled. In this sense he is very much like Lear's beloved Fool. Alleyn concludes, "he's only dumb nor'-nor'-west and yesterday, I fancy, the wind was in the south."[26] Ernie's major problem lies in distinguishing appearance and reality.

When the dance of the swords leads to a decapitation without the mythic rebirth of the traditional performances, Alleyn enters, full of enough Shakespearean lore and knowledge of folk motifs to brighten the lives of Dr. Otterly and Camilla with the depth of his understanding.

He knows mummery too. "The ritual death of the Fool is the old mystery of sacrifice, isn't it, with the promise of renewal behind it?" Alleyn asks perceptively.[27] The doctor and the detective recite the numerous phrases that come out of folk drama: "Mounting one's hobby-horse! Horseplay! Playing the fool! Cutting capers! Midsummer madness! Very possibly 'horn mad.'"[28] Alleyn immediately identifies *King Lear* as an outgrowth of the dance theme, making Otterly a very happy fellow. When they move on to discussing superstitions, Alleyn holds that everyone has some, "Cossetted but reluctantly acknowleged. Like the bastard sons of Shakspearian [sic] papas."[29]

Otterly admits that he feels it is unlucky to see blood. When the murder occurs, it is relatively bloodless, and no suspect is blood-spattered, even though, as Simon Begg points out:

> the assailant in such cases is well-enough bloodied to satisfy the third murderer in Macbeth.[30]

When Fox identifies a Shakespearean quotation, Alleyn says:

> This case smacks of the Elizabethan. And I don't altogether mean *Hamlet* or *Lear*....But those earlier plays of violence when people kill each other in a sort of quintessence of spleen and other people cheer each other up by saying things like, "And now my lord, to leave these doleful dumps."[31]

Marsh continues the parallels when the dancers reenact the performance, and the torches make a strange effect: "Like the setting for a barbaric play—*King Lear*, perhaps."[32] A form of barbarous disrespect for human life triggers the crime. William Andersen died—not because he deserved his death—by trying to reject progress—but because the killer had a perfect opportunity to commit the murder. The senseless cruelty inflicted is like that of Goneril and Regan in *Lear*. The victim was indeed more sinned against than sinning.

Death of a Peer parallels *Macbeth* (it even has what might be called three witches), both in terms of the family situation and in the solution of the crime. The Lamprey family's talent is in living well. Actually none of them have much common sense, as the world defines it, except young Mike (who wants to be a policeman). They have been living off an inheritance from a deceased aunt, a temporary situation which does not put them in the best light during the murder investigation involving their unloved and unloving relative. Gabriel, Marquis of Wutherwood and Rune, is Lord Charles's wealthy, though unpleasant, older brother.

At the beginning of the story, the family has gone broke, but sees their fortunes rise again when they receive a good offer for their New Zealand estate. They set sail for England with the intention of increasing their financial status. Although they are actually quite poor, they attempt to capitalize on their name and style in order to obtain credit and dodge the bill collectors. By the time Roberta Grey moves to England to live with her aunt after her parents have been killed, the Lampreys are desperately in need of money, which they attempt to borrow from rich Uncle Gabriel. His wife, a self-proclaimed "witch" in her fifties, is fat, sallow, and artificially painted.

The Lampreys' visit, which begins amicably enough, results in a heated argument between the two brothers, and ends with Lord Gabriel in the elevator with a skewer through his eye. Lady Katherine Lobe, eccentric and deaf, is suspected when she disappears and reappears again with the happy news that all the Lamprey's financial problems have been solved. Her wild appearance adds to the news of the bizarre death. Two "weird sisters" have now made their appearance.

Young Henry will now become Lord Rune[33] and his ascent from poor aristocrat to the family title and fortune is comparable to the change of title in *Macbeth*. The death of one titled man has lead to the advancement for the father and son of the Lamprey family. Since Aunt V. has become obsessed with witchcraft, the playful youngsters act rather like witches themselves. Frid croaks:

> Weary se'nnights nine times nine
> Shall he dwindle, peak and pine
> Double, double toil and trouble;
> Fire burn, and cauldron bubble.[34]

She ignores Henry's reminder that she told them it was unlucky to quote from *Macbeth*.

Alleyn also senses the parallel with *Macbeth*. When Lady Wutherford laughs, Alleyn thinks that it is:

> ...for all the world like the cackle of one of the witches in a traditional rendering of Macbeth.[35]

As she moves her finger across her lips, he remembers:

> You seem to understand me
> By each at once, her choppy fingers laying
> Upon her skinny lips.[36]

He tells Fox that he is uneasy: "Pricking of the thumbs or something."[37] Although the *Comedy of Errors* is twice mentioned[38] because of the confusion surrounding the Lamprey twins who switch identities, *Macbeth* is the underlying play within this novel.

In Chapter 16, "Night Thickens," the pieces of the puzzle come together. Henry is reading *Macbeth*, noting that the Bard "has a number of very meaty things to say about murder."[39] Although Stephen thinks it "bad form" to read *Macbeth*, Frid intones:

> Night thickens
> And the crow makes wing to the rooky
>   wood:
> Good things of the day begin to droop and
>   drowse,

> While night's black agents to their preys do
> rouse.[40]

As Alleyn walks home by Westminster Bridge, a constable on duty passes and greets his famous superior with:

> It's a thick night. Have you ever read a
> play called "Macbeth," sir?

The one by Shakespeare, he adds. He was exposed to the work at the Old Vic, found it morbid and not his usual type of entertainment, but compelling enough that he obtained a copy and began reading it. He recalls the words as he walks through the stormy night. Although heaths and woods may not describe a huge city, he is haunted by the words. Night thickens; birds fly through trees; and, Alleyn completes

> While night's black agents to their prey do
> rouse.[41]

The lines have impact. The constable observes that the Macbeths, like many modern crooks, are superstitious.

> They were a very nasty couple. Bad
> type....She was the worst of the two, in my
> opinion. Tried to fix the job so's it's look as
> if the servants had done it....I reckon if he
> hadn't lost his nerve they'd have got away
> with it.[42]

The ideas planted by that strange literary interlude in the dead of night, with a man removed from the case, set an important tone.

Alleyn is under unusual pressure to solve the case, and his tension is not eased when Fox finds a doll, melted and misshapened, dressed like the late lord and stabbed in the chest with a long pin, another obvious sign of his widow's hatred in the form of witchcraft. *The Com-*

pendium Maleficorum holds pride of place in Lady Wutherwood's bedroom, and includes a frequently-read chapter on soporific spells. The usually watchful night nurse snores heavily, her sleep induced by a morphia tablet added to her cocoa. When Robin hears noises in the night, then recognizes a shadowy figure with a candle as Lady Wutherwood, she is convinced evil is afoot.

Bill Giggle, the chauffeur, is the second victim. He was engaged to Tinkerton, Lady Wutherwood's maid, and he had just inherited an attractive cottage, promised to him long ago in appreciation for his father's having saved the previous lord's life....The motive for Giggle's death is uncertain.

The night nurse, when roused at last, assists the constable on duty to search for the missing Lady Wutherwood, who fights him off violently when discovered. The expected knife is not recovered, but the severed hand of another person is found in milady's pocket. The nurse faints, and the unstable widow, whom everyone admits is "a bit dotty" quickly becomes a prime suspect. Her *Compendium Maleficorum* opens naturally to a chapter on "The Hand of Glory," and Lady Wutherwood's handwriting in the margins seems to underscore her guilt in the matter.

But Alleyn has doubts about the seemingly devoted Tinkerton:

> I fancy Tinkerton, like Lady Macbeth, was the brains of the party, and I may add that a casual conversation with a Shakespearian P.C. first gave me the idea.[43]

Tinkerton, it seems, had driven her lover to kill Lord Wutherwood in order to inherit the cottage, and she stood by to finish the job if he failed. Alleyn was convinced that she had done something to distract anyone who came near at the time the murder was being committed ("Faint, like Lady Macbeth"),[44] and that she in turn killed Giggle because he was growing uncomfortable with the thought of having committed murder. Tinkerton was the one who planted the idea of using the Hand of Glory to keep everyone in the house under its spell in Lady Wuther-wood's mind. Thus consciously or unconsciously, the murder plot indeed drew heavily from *Macbeth*, and the solution was forthcoming when an uninvolved police constable innocently brought the parallels to Alleyn's attention. (The Jove edition of *Death of a Peer* contains a blurb which states

> ...with a "sidekick" named Shakespeare, Inspector Alleyn singles out a killer from a glittering array of suspects.)

Another mystery solved with some help from the Bard is *Scales of Justice*, in which "The Rape of Lucrece" provides some clues. Colonel Carterette and his daughter Rose are smitten with the Elizabethan dramatists, and their conversations about poetry combine with a murder perpetrated on the banks of a river where the victim had been fishing. The fish found near Carterette's body was the legendary "Old One" which had been caught by Octavius Danberry-Phinn at almost exactly the same time as the murder was taking place. A search for the correct catch reveals the imprint of golf shoe spikes which betrays the murderer. The possibility that the direction the river flows has had something to do with the way the catch was switched reminds Alleyn of "The Rape of Lucrece": "There's a bit about the Avon at Clopton Bridge, but it might have been written about the Chyne at this very point."[45]

> As through an arch the violent roaring tide
> Outruns the eye that doth behold his haste,
> Yet in the eddy boundeth in his pride
> Back to the strait that forced him
>   on so fast.[46]

Of all the Shakespearean plays and poems to which Marsh refers in her works, none is quoted so frequently as *Macbeth*. The phrases, "Double, double, toil and trouble" and "By the pricking of my thumbs, something wicked this way comes" are nearly as familiar to the English-speaking world as "Friends, Romans, Countrymen" and "To be or not to be." *Macbeth* certainly is one of the best known of all dramatic works, successful not only in and of itself, but in its many successful and brilliant variations, such as Akira Kurosawa's *pastiche* Japanese film, *Throne of Blood.* It has an elemental appeal to those who blame their lack of success on the person who is perceived as standing in the way. Equally affected are wives and lovers who also long for a loved one's advancement enough to perform dire deeds of evil in his or her name.

    Death of a Peer, as we have seen, is loosely patterned on the play itself. *Light Thickens* takes place during a production of the work; Millicent Ancred, a middle-aged homemaker with no flair for drama (although her name is taken from an eighteenth century comedy and is suggestive of deviousness). She kills to advance her son Cedric, who has little ambition of his own, and who is one of the more successful members of his family as it is. Constance Cartell, of *Hand in Glove*, kills to protect her beloved niece; Cressida Tottenham, of *Tied Up in Tinsel*, murders her own father in order to retain her illusion of nobility; Harry Grove of *Killer Dolphin* kills to preserve his own reputation. *Macbeth* thus is a classic symbol of the human drive to succeed at any cost. It is not a matter of greed so much as it is power, and the maintaining of one's proper position in the scheme of things.

    In *A Man Lay Dead*, Charles Rankin has made life miserable for Arthur Wilde since Eton, bullying and teasing him unmercifully, and carrying on an affair openly with Wilde's wife. The final straw is when Rankin embarrasses Wilde in front of his wife at a party. The only way Wilde can see to reestablish his bruised ego is to remove the obstacle. As the witches materialize on stage to predict Macbeth's hidden desires, Sir Hubert Handesley presents Arthur with a murder game scenario which gives him the perfect opportunity to carry out his hidden desire.

    In *Enter a Murderer*, Felix Gardener responds to Nigel's suggestion that he get some sleep with Macbeth's troubled words: "Sleep that knits up the ravelled sleeve of

care,"[47] thus beginning Marsh's pattern of quoting or refer-
ring to *Macbeth*. In *Died in the Wool*, Flossie, who inter-
feres with a German spy, hints at her knowledge: "She'd
pull an arch face and, for all the world like one of the
weird sisters in *Macbeth*, she'd lay her rather choppy finger
on her lips and say: 'But we mustn't be indiscreet, must
we?'"[48]

References to the unlucky habit of quoting from
Macbeth appear in: *Death in a White Tie*,[49] *Death of a
Peer*,[50] *Overture to Death*,[51] and forms a large portion of
the *Light Thickens* plot. "By the pricking of my thumbs"
appears in *Death and the Dancing Footman*,[52] *Dead Water*,[53] and *Death at the Bar*.[54] In *Clutch of Constables*
which focuses more on the art world, the Hewsons had seen
a performance of *Macbeth* at Stratford-on-Avon, an appropriate entertainment for Ed and Sally-Lou Moran, who are
American criminals. Mr. Merryman asks for the source of
Alleyn's quotation about an "art to find the mind's con-
struction in the face," and is told that it is from "Macbeth,
one, four Duncan on Cawdor."[55] George Pastern complains: "Ask a couple of people to dine and your mother
behaves like Lady Macbeth."[56]

In *Dead Water* beautiful, guilt-ridden, Mrs. Barrimore walks about wringing her hands. At first Alleyn
thinks the source is inappropriate when he finds the quotation springing to his mind: "Look what she does now. See
how she rubs her hands!" On the same wave length, Miss
Emily replies: "It is an accustomed action with her to seem
thus washing her hands."[57] Later Mrs. Barrimore is more
in control, but still, "Her hands writhed together."[58] Alleyn learns that inadvertently she had caused a death when
her lover hid their secret by eliminating a witness.

In *Final Curtain* the victim poses for his last portrait
in his *Macbeth* costume. Much is made of his experience
with the unlucky play. Troy rereads the play in preparation
for her work, and, ironically, Cedric, who is inadvertently
the hoped-for parallel to Macbeth's rise to power, declares
that *Macbeth* is an attrociously bad play. The Siddons'
room has a steel engraving of Sarah Siddons (of Lady Macbeth fame), the sister of Charles and John Philip Kemble,

and of Charles' daughter, Fanny. The Kembles were once prominent among nineteenth century Shakespearean players, a real-life theatrical family comparable in many respects to the fictional Ancreds. Sarah's portrayal of Lady Macbeth has incluenced subsequent actresses' interpretation of the role.

Troy's portrait of the elderly actor is brilliant; as Cedric says: "It really *is* theatre and the Old Person and that devastating Bard all synthesized and made eloquent and everything."59 When he takes his father's place so he can rest, Cedric wears theatrical makeup in order to "get the feeling of the Macsoforth *seeping* through into every fold of the mantle."60 Troy feels that she has not painted Macbeth but "an old actor looking backwards into his realization of the part. Would they see that the mood was one of the relinquishment?"61 *Macbeth*, then, underscores the story of a proud old man and a family that, in spite of its constant fighting, still loves him.

One character describes Sir Henry's daughter Pauline thusly:

> Since the Tragedy she is almost indistinguishable from Lady Macduff. Or perhaps that frightful Shakespearian dowager who courses her way up hill and down dale through one of the historical dramas."62

But his children and his young fiancée would no more have killed Sir Henry than Duncan's family would have destroyed the kindly Scots king to get to the throne. A misguided outsider with the perfect opportunity provided by a position of trust brought Sir Henry to an unnecessary end.

Light Thickens tells us more about the production of *Macbeth* than it does about Inspector Alleyn. Following two successful and accident-free productions of *Macbeth*, Peregrine Jay will not listen to the superstitions that Nina Gaythorn and others pass on to him. Even *My Fair Lady* proved unlucky for Rex Harrison, he notes skeptically, when the actor's hairpiece caught in a chandelier and was whisked up to the "flies." Nina has a whole ritual of purification based on the superstitions of four generations of theater people.

Although Jay does not accept the idea of "bad luck," he works hard to create an aura of oppressiveness and evil about the set. A rag-covered skeleton dangles from a gallows on a high stone platform. The costumes are heavy and primitive. Looming over all is Gaston Sears with his *claideamh-mor*, known to everyone but the omniscient Alleyn as a "claymore." Even when Jay is injured by the wooden claymore with which Macbeth and Macduff are practicing, he refuses to accept that the play is unlucky.

A Maori, Rangi Western, plays a witch—one of three nice young actors who have been transformed into the embodiment of evil. His "tiki," tales of his cannibal ancestors, and his extremely effective stage business of weaving a spell, enhance the supernatural tone. A raging storm not only panics one of the witches, Blondie, but also destroys an old building nearby. The enormously realistic mask of Banquo, with blood running from its open mouth, appears in unexpected places, frightening the actors. A dead rat materializes in Rangi's "witch's bag."

Ominous words suit the actions. A message to the front office announces that there is a murderer's son in the cast. Young William Smith is a model child, and a fine actor as well. His father, however, is known as "The Hampstead Chopper," and had decapitated five women three years earlier. One of the "Chopper's" victims was Bruce Barrabell's wife. After all of these sinister happenings, even sensible Peregrine "Perry" Jay finds himself crossing his fingers. The opening night is a success, with royalty in attendance—but Perry trips over some light cables, falls flat on his face—and discovers Props as drunk as the Porter of the play.

Sir Dougal Macdougal is decapitated during a performance, and the actors begin juggling for star positions. During a reenactment (at which Alleyn demonstrates how familiar he is with the play) Gaston Sears, the understudy, plays Macbeth and begins to envision himself in the starring role. Perry, however, brings the play to a close—and revives his own drama *about* Shakespeare, *The Glove*—when

Alleyn points out that capitalizing on such horrible incidents to attract larger audiences is "an insult to a beautiful production."[63]

Gaston Sears' motive for murder is simply that it was "convenient." Sir Dougal had baited and insulted him, as Charles Rankin had insulted Arthur Wilde in *A Man Lay Dead*. Thus the murders in Marsh's first and last novels have similar motivations. Alleyn holds that the play *Macbeth* had unduly influenced people. There's a

> ...stepped-up abnormality about the whole thing [he tells Fox], as if the actors had become motivated by the play.[64]

The dark mood obviously drove Sears from his precariously eccentric but harmless state over the line into insanity. He truly believed that the claymore thirsted for blood. The power of evil belonged to *Macbeth*.

Quotations from Shakespeare's plays range from playful exclamations to piercing revelation of character. Marsh compares at least two "old maid" victims with the character of Ophelia—with hair floating on the water—although neither of the deaths (one in *Dead Water*, the other in *A Clutch of Constables*) is a suicide. Most of Marsh's Shakespearean quotations come to her as naturally as metaphors do to other writers. The circumstances of the plays cited usually bear some relationship to the plots of the novels in which they are quoted. Following is a list of Shakespearean plays and the Marsh novels which contain quotes from them.

The average detective is not noted for his Shakespearean quotations (although the average producer-director *may* be able to quote her favorite author!). One explanation for Inspector Alleyn's predilection for references from the Bard is the obvious one—that Alleyn is the well-educated second son of a peer with experience in the diplomatic corps. Another is that Alleyn is an admitted connoisseur of drama. He has a friend who is often assigned the task of critiquing plays, and he has thus become the Yard's in-house specialist on things dramatic. Finally, in Alleyn's own words:

> Over the years of that soul-destroying non-activity known to the Force as keeping obbo, when the facility for razor-sharp perception must cut through the drag of bodily discomfort and boredom, Alleyn had developed a technique of self-discipline. He hunted through his memory for odd bits from his favourite author that, in however cockeyed a fashion, could be said to refer to his job. As: "O me! When eyes hath Love put in my head. Which have no correspondence with true sight." And: "Mad slanderers by mad ears believed be." And: "Hence, though suborn'd informer," which came in very handy when some unreliable snout let the police-side down.
>
> This frivolous pastime had led indirectly to the memorizing of certain sonnets. Now, when with his eyes streaming and his arm giving him hell, he had embarked upon "The expense of spirit in a waste of shame," he saw, though his peephole, a faint light.[65]

So the "blurb" for *Death of a Peer* seems accurate: Alleyn really does have a sidekick named Shakespeare who keeps him sane, good-spirited, and shrewd in his character observations.

APPENDIX II

SHAKESPEAREAN PLAYS AND THE
NGAIO MARSH NOVELS WHICH QUOTE THEM

ANTONY AND CLEOPATRA: *When in Rome*; *Singing in the Shrouds*; *Tied Up in Tinsel*

AS YOU LIKE IT: *Final Curtain*

A COMEDY OF ERRORS: *A Clutch of Constables*; *Death of a Peer*

HAMLET: *A Clutch of Constables*; *Colour Scheme*; *Dead Water*; *Death in Ecstasy*; *Died in the Wool*; *Enter a Murderer*; *False Scent*; *Grave Mistake*; *The Nursing Home Murder*; *Vintage Murder*; *A Wreath for Rivera*

HENRY IV, PARTS 1-2: *Grave Mistake*; *Night at the Vulcan*; *Photo Finish*

HENRY V: *Colour Scheme*; *Night at the Vulcan*

JULIUS CAESAR: *Enter a Murderer*

KING LEAR: *Death of a Fool*; *False Scent*; *Final Curtain*; *Tied Up in Tinsel*; *When in Rome*

MACBETH: *A Clutch of Constables*; *Dead Water*; *Death and the Dancing Footman*; *Death in a White Tie*; *Death of a Peer*; *Died in the Wool*; *Enter a Murderer*; *Final Curtain*; *Light Thickens*; *The Nursing Home Murder*; *Overture to Death*; *Singing in the Shrouds*; *Spinsters in Jeopardy*

THE MERCHANT OF VENICE: *Hand in Glove*

A MIDSUMMER NIGHT'S DREAM: *Death in a White Tie*; *Death of a Peer*; *Light Thickens*

MUCH ADO ABOUT NOTHING: *Artists in Crime*; *Died in the Wool*; *Overture to Death*

OTHELLO: *Black as He's Painted*; *Death in a White Tie*; *Final Curtain*; *Photo Finish*; *Scales of Justice*

ROMEO AND JULIET: *Hand in Glove*; *Last Ditch*; *Scales of Justice*; *When in Rome*

THE TAMING OF THE SHREW: *Night at the Vulcan*

THE TEMPEST: *Black as He's Painted*; *Spinsters in Jeopardy*; *Tied Up in Tinsel*

V.

BACK STAGE

THEATRICAL DEVICES IN MARSH'S FICTION

Earl Bargainnier and George Grella have noted that the dramatic structure of Marsh's novels include prostasis, epistasis, and catastrophe, with a short closing summary. Setting, characters, and mood build over a long period before the initial murder, followed by a series of dramatic "confrontations" between Inspector Alleyn and various witnesses and suspects. The facts are presented and summarized by Nigel or Fox, then synthesized by Alleyn into a concise explanation of how and why the murder took place. Marsh skillfully merges dialogue, local color and interesting action into a cohesive whole. The crimes which take place in her novels are rarely simple, nor are the motives.

In fact, Marsh's novels have a great deal in common with the old periodical or pulp serials which in turn greatly resemble scenes in a drama. The popular Saturday morning matinees were sometimes called "chapter plays," and Marsh has assimilated such page-turning action into her works. Chapters usually conclude on a high note of dramatic surprise or unanswered questions, keeping her readers eager to find out what happens next. Such conclusions might almost be termed "curtain" lines. Concluding chapter lines from *Artists in Crime* is a case in point (although any other novel might yield similar examples):

CHAPTER I. Alleyn equivocates ironically about his feelings for Agatha Troy: "*...I've got nothing at all for Miss Troy, and I can assure you she has got even less than that for me.*"

CHAPTER II. Lady Alleyn asks Troy's age, and indicates that she is aware that her son is in love, seriously and permanently.

CHAPTER III. Valmai Seacliff announces that she and Basil Pilgrim are engaged, thus dropping a bombshell.

CHAPTER IV. Alleyn says goodbye "for the moment" to Troy.

CHAPTER V. Cedric Malmsley announces that (just after they had looked at a portrait of Sonia) Garcia had asked him if he had "*ever felt like killing [his] mistress just for the horror of doing it.*"

CHAPTER VI. Troy admits that every artist had felt like killing Sonia. Sonia had ruined Troy's superb painting of Valmai Seacliff out of sheer spite.

CHAPTER VII. "*Troy made an impressive exit.*"

CHAPTER VIII. "*Unerring as ever, Mr. Alleyn,*" says Nigel, walking into the room and surprising Alleyn with a good line.

CHAPTER IX. "*It's only that the girl Sonia was going to have a kid, and Pilgrim's the father. So now what?*"

CHAPTER X. "*The fatal woman is going to be very sick.*"

CHAPTER XI. Bobbie O'Dawne's letter reveals her fear of Garcia, hints at possibilities of unpleasant secrets, and indicates that Sonia has been asking for trouble.

CHAPTER XII. Alleyn, Fox, and Nigel are stumped. How did Garcia remove his gear and vanish if he had been under the influence of alcohol and drugs?

CHAPTER XIII. Simply good night, but Lady Alleyn indicates her understanding of Troy's strange behavior around Alleyn.

CHAPTER XIV. Goodbye and thank you to Troy, who is becoming more civil to the Inspector.

CHAPTER XV. Bobbie expresses feelings that Garcia is gone for good.

CHAPTER XVI. Alleyn tells Fox (but not the reader) why he is on the way to Brixton, a typical Marsh strategy. *"Sit down for a minute...and I'll tell you,"* Alleyn says; and there the chapter ends.

CHAPTER XVII. Garcia's death was not suicide or accident, but murder, Alleyn announces.

CHAPTER XVIII. Alleyn teases Nigel about spending his days with ladies of the chorus. He employs his "Watson" as a spy once more.

CHAPTER XIX. Without explaining why to his onlookers, Alleyn announces that if the tumbler has only Pilgrim's prints, *"we'll be within sight of an arrest."*

CHAPTER XX. In the penultimate chapter ending, Alleyn confronts the killer. *"I arrest you for the murder of Wolf Garcia on..."*

CHAPTER XXI. Troy admits that she "nearly" loves Alleyn.

Each of these conclusions is a "curtain line," either a bombshell, a teaser about what Alleyn is not yet explaining, or an important clue. The chapter endings are set up in the same way as scenes in a play—with just a hint of more to come once the curtain rises again. Even at the conclusion the last act promises the Troy/Alleyn love affair will continue with the next novel.

Most of these mysteries also include a few character types who have importance to the plot, but are neither victims nor killers. These roles are presented in the same manner as the dramatic "cameo" roles we've become accustomed to seeing on stage and screen. Mrs. Bünz, the folk drama fanatic in *Death of a Fool*, will fight through blizzards, freeze while she spies on rehearsals, lecture on her favorite topic, and negotiate her way into a heavy costume (which bruises her shoulders). She is, as the actress Camilla Campion observes, a fine example of the stock "character." Cressida Tottenham of *Tied Up in Tinsel*, Bobbie O'Dawne in *Artists in Crime*, and Sonia Orrincourt of *Final Curtain* are the stereotypical empty-headed, gold-digging chorus girls. Bohemian artists of limited talent but unlimited egotism appear in *Last Ditch* and *Artists in Crime*. Other stock characters include: the horrid child actor; the religious "con" man; the sweet young girl and the earnest young man who fall in love; the eccentric old lady; the sexually frustrated middle-aged lady; and the effeminate actor. The "ugly American" shows up in *Death in Ecstasy*.

A true stock character who appears often enough to be considered an individual is Mr. Rattisbon, the family lawyer who specializes in wills. In *The Nursing Home Murder* he is given a Shavian description:

> ...[Fox] signed and went out, returning to ush-er in Mr. James Rattisbon of Knightley, Knightley and Rattisbon, uncle to Lady O'-Callaghan and solicitor to the deceased and his family. Mr. Rattisbon was one of those elderly solicitors whose appearance explains why the expression "dried-up" is so inevitably applied by novelists to men of law. He was desiccated. He was dressed in clothes of a dated type that looked rather shabby, but were actually in good repair. He wore a winged collar, rather high, and a dark tie, rather narrow. He was discreetly bald, somewhat blind, and a little tremulous. He had a kind of quick stuttering utterance, and

a curious trick of thrusting out his pointed tongue and rattling it exceedingly rapidly between his thin lips. This may have served as an antidote to the stutter or it may have signified a kind of professional relish. His hands were bird-like claws with very large purplish veins. It was impossible to picture him in any sort of domestic surroundings.[1]

Alleyn describes him as doing "his incredibly classical portrait of the family lawyer by putting together the tips of his fingers.[2] In *Death in Ecstasy* he calls him a "...desiccated, tittuppy, nice old fuss-pot. Gives one the idea that he is a good actor slightly overdoing his part."[3] "Rats" is still practicing, and as sterotyped as ever in *Final Curtain*. He is a Victorian era inheritor of the profession of dealing with the estates of upper middle-class people. He is shrewd, reliable, honest, and a real help to Alleyn in his understanding of people as well as their wills.

In addition to characters who might be found in plays, the actual plays themselves are used as plot devices in the novels. *Enter a Murderer* finds the murderer and his victim on stage in *The Rat and the Beaver*, a suspense drama. Though Gardener and Surbonadier are both fine actors, the death scene is *too* "realistic," as Alleyn, a spectator, notes. The "Rat-and-the-Beaver" game, he quickly discovers, has been going on both on-stage and off. Even before Alleyn learns all the facts, however, he recognizes genuine emotional reactions even when they are portrayed by talented actors during the performance:

The report of the revolver, anticipated by every nerve in the audience, was deafeningly loud. Surbonadier crumpled up and, turning a face that was blank of every expression but that of profound astonishment, fell in a heap at Gardener's feet. So far the acting honours in the scene had been even, but now Felix Gardener surpassed anything that had gone before. His face reflected, horribly, the sur-

> prise on Surbonadier's. He stood looking
> foolishly at the gun in his hand and then let it
> fall to the floor. He turned, bewildered, and
> peered at the audience as though asking a
> question. He looked at the stage exits as if
> he meditated an escape. Then he gazed at
> Stephanie Vaughan, who, in her turn, was
> looking with horror from him to what he had
> done.[4]

When they speak they seem to be talking machines rather than actors as their discipline cuts through their shock. Although the audience is overwhelmed with the quality of the "acting," Alleyn dashes for backstage and begins his investigation.

This novel sets a precedent for Marsh's characteristic "murders in front of an audience" device so unique to her works. Murder occurs off stage during a performance of *Macbeth* in *Light Thickens* and during the "Dance of the Five Sons" in *Death of a Fool*. After his final scene, and just before the curtain call, Clark Bennington dies in *Night at the Vulcan*. His killer commits suicide that same evening when he realizes that Alleyn has solved the case but is trying not to cause him to be humilitated in public.

Marsh does not allow the performance to end just because someone's life does. It is after almost everyone has left the theater that the murders occur in *Killer Dolphin* and *Photo Finish*. The drama never has a chance to commence when the pianist is shot to death as she begins playing Rachmaninoff's *Prelude in C-Sharp Minor* in *Overture to Death*. The house is packed. But the production is amateurish and poorly done—so Marsh does not force this "show to go on."

Other deaths occur in public: Carlos Rivera falls during the "Hot Guy, Hot Gunner" number in *Wreath for Rivera*, giving the murderer a perfect opportunity to kill him. During an evening church service, beautiful Cara Quanyne gibbers, speaks in tongues, claps and rocks to and fro, as she reaches for the wine in a ceremonial cup. Then she twitches and is still, thus the title of *Death in Ecstasy*.

A similar religious-like ceremony results in the death of the Honorable Grizel Locke in *Spinsters in Jeopardy*. Though the murder and drug trafficking which take place in the village are serious, the final ceremony is comic. Something goes wrong when the very masculine Raoul Milano replaces Ginny Taylor as "the "Bride" and Alleyn somehow becomes one of the "votaries" in a staged act, a contrived showdown which would actually make quite good theater.

In *Black as He's Painted* the Ng'gombwanian ambassador is speared to death at a diplomatic reception in front of the Alleyns, with guards, diplomats and dignitaries in attendance, but no one sees (or will admit to seeing) the killer. Similarly, the lights go out for a murder with an inn full of witnesses in *Death at the Bar*. Here, a dark virtuoso employs the "round the clock" trick in a busy pub and in front of witnesses who are watching his every move.

A tour group in *When in Rome* discusses the cult of Mithras and its ritual sacrifices while listening to Barnaby Grant reading from his best-selling book *Simon in Latium*, which is set on the very spot where they are standing. Suddenly the lights go out and Mailer and Violetta (the strange postcard vendor who had just created a scene) vanish. Later they are discovered, quite dramatically, one in a sarcophagus and the other trapped by a foot caught in a grate at the bottom of a well. Alleyn's crawl down to the bottom of the well to investigate is an exploit worthy of Bulldog Drummond.

Parties in Marsh become a full-fledged art form. From the first mystery on, Marsh used the "deadly house-party" as a key scene in her plots. Of all her books, *Death and the Dancing Footman* may be the crowning example of this technique.

Set in 1940, the novel revolves around Jonathan Royal who has organized a weekend party in the manner of Pirandello in *Six Characters in Search of an Author*. Royal has confined seven people who have reason to hate each other in a small space, made even smaller by a serendipitous snowstorm, just so he can observe their conversations and actions-as if the party were a "slice-of-life" drama. He

uses various flowers to symbolize the types of characters—
a grand dame, an ingenue, a femme fatale, rival brothers, a
beauty specialist, and a classic "heavy." Aubrey Mandrake, a successful verse dramatist, recognizes how Royal
proposes to use the situation to "create" a drama by confin-
ing his captive audience on his "stage" and argues that
Jonathan has "invited stark murder" or "some disastrous
vaudeville show" to his house.5 The murder takes place
during the gathering, and the murderer is in the midst of
them all!

Alleyn tests his theory by forcing the killer to par-
ticipate in a reenactment of his crime. From his interviews
Alleyn has the information he needs. Instead of merely
telling how he solved the puzzle, Alleyn walks the people
through the process. Mandrake finds it a horrible experience: "We're creating it all over again. It's as if we were
making something take form."6 The trapped murderer's
clever booby traps lead inevitably to his own downfall.

In *Final Curtain* Sir Henry Ancred has a beautiful
annual birthday celebration which Troy describes in dramatic terms as:

> ...the big scene from a film script....She [is]
> the bit part lady....Where else but on the
> screen was such opulence to be found....
> Never out of a film studio had characters
> been so well-typed.

The regular guests and the neighboring squire are

> ...carefully selected cameo parts, too like
> themselves to be credible.7

It's a "great Family Act," Cedric Ancred tells her, in which
they, as family members pretend the way actors do on
stage. "People that hate each other's guts make love like
angels.8

Troy's portrait of Sir Henry is unveiled, causing her
to have first night jitters over the family's reactions to the
painting. There is a brief moment during which the muti-

lated portrait introduces a comic note, but Troy manages to clean off the flying cow over Macbeth's (Henry's) head with her usual cool efficiency.

There is a careful outline to be followed each year at Sir Henry's party. He sets his house in order, discusses his latest will, makes speeches of gratitude, and inveighs against current practices of his family members. He is a temperamental, easily outraged old man. When he learns that two of his cousins intend to marry each other he goes into a tantrum. With her sharp artist's eye for detail, Troy observes:

> Old lips, shaking with rage, old eyes whose fierceness was glazed by rheum, old hands that jerked in uncoordinated fury; these were intolerable manifestations of emotion.[9]

But Sir Henry does not see himself as anything but the soul of magnanimity. Pleased with himself he thinks:

> Such frankness was perhaps out of fashion nowadays but it had an appropriate Shakespearean precedent. King Lear—but glancing at his agonized daughters Sir Henry did not pursue the analogy.[10]

The experienced actor should have remembered that at a similar family gathering King Lear made equally hasty judgments—with equally appalling repercussions.

The people with whom Sir Henry, like Lear, was most angry had not been unloving or disloyal. It is, on the contrary, his own desire to wield his power over his heirs by making and remaking his wills which causes Sir Henry's downfall. In view of the bickering over the engagement, the general hostility toward Sonia, and the practical jokes which demean a distinguished old actor, any civility at this party is amazing. The family's hostility is muted, though serving champagne and hot crayfish, both of which are on the proscribed list for a gentleman with gastroenteritis, is a consciously destructive act, setting up the murder to look like a fatal attack of a long-standing disease.

The murder game that inspired *A Man Lay Dead* (and possibly a whole career of mystery writing) is carried on at another house party composed of people bound to generate conflict and action. Although Sir Hubert Handesley's parties are famous for surprises, a real murder was not on the agenda. An equally deadly party occurs in *Vintage Murder* when, following a performance of *Ladies of Leisure*, the entire company, staff, local people, and Alleyn witness a jeroboam of wine as it crushes the head of the honorée's husband.

The period *after* a party or performance is also a dangerous time in the world of Marsh's novels. Following the Maori's party in *Colour Scheme* a scream is heard and the ominous sound of boiling mud. The victim's identity remains hidden for some time, since the sinister pool leaves few traces. Following her birthday party—and a series of obnoxious tantrums, Mary Bellamy receives her last fatal drenching of what she believes to be perfume. Her guests are still gathered around waiting for her to open the gifts she will never see. On his way home from a gala coming-out party Lord Robert Gospell, who is a welcome guest at any social gathering, shares a cab with an old friend—who kills him with professional ease. In *Wreath for Rivera* a dinner party held before the nightclub debut of Lord Pastern generates several motives for murdering the accordion-playing Carlos Rivera.

Two parties take place in *Singing in the Shrouds*. When the group goes ashore for a gala evening at Las Palmas, Mrs. Dillington-Blick dons the Spanish-style dress which marks her for murder and is given a doll with a broken neck as a prelude to that act. At both parties Alleyn carefully observes the reaction of people to his leading statements—and watches for the killer to betray his identity.

The production in *Tied Up in Tinsel* is a normal part of the Christmas celebration at the Halberds. Friends, neighbors, and relatives gather to expand a houseparty to a festive celebration of the primitive roots of the season. The

Druid wears a golden costume as the precursor of the winter solstice. Hillary Bill-Tasman's delightful Aunt Bed and Uncle Flea are as excited about the Teutonic and Druidical myths as he is. Even Cressida becomes "wrapped up" in the party, for which she becomes stage manager. Her costume, a skin tight gold-lamé trouser suit, is very like the Druid's in color and texture, although his is wide-sleeved and enveloping, an important factor in Alleyn's solution later.

People involved in the production suffer the same jitters of any first night performer. The Druid enters, but does not remove his gloves as he is directed to do emphatically during the rehearsal. He is impressive in his role. Insiders learn later that Uncle Flea has had an attack which prevented him from going on, and Alfred Moult, his valet, is persuaded to take his place at the last minute. Moult had imbibed heavily enough of the holiday "spirits" to disclose to Cressida that he was her father. During all the confusion, Cressida kills Moult, dons his costume, takes his place as the Druid, disposes of the body, and returns casually to the party. Moult's indiscretion precipitated his demise under cover of a houseful of suspects-including a staff consisting of convicted murderers!

In *Dead Water* the interior "drama" is a typical local tourist pageant, a project of the local Drama Circle. A dumpy, unattractive girl is chosen to represent the ethereally beautiful "Green Lady." The malfunctioning microphone is badly used by Miss Cost, who speaks into it only occasionally, when her words are picked up "savagely" and flung "upon the heavy air." When she does not speak into it she changes "into a voiceless puppet that opened and shut its mouth, cast up its eyes and waved its arms."11 The lyrics of the choir's song are strained ("was wroughten"); the large blonde girl representing the Green Lady loses her beads; and a tremendous storm creates a stampede which destroys all further efforts towards dramatic elevation.

In *Death of a Peer* the Lamprey children present an equally unsuccessful performance—a charade about Jael and Sisera. The skewer used as a prop becomes the murder weapon, but the charade is comically overacted, almost as ridiculous as the escapades of Bottom and company in *A Midsummer Night's Dream*. In fact the children actually recite lines from the parodic love scene of Bottom and Titania. Their foolish little game prefigures the ugly death of Lord Wutherford, who sees no humor in the charade whatsoever.

Several other books are based around a "performance" which is in reality an elaborately-staged party. *Hand in Glove* features an April Fool's Day treasure hunt given by the flamboyant Lady Désirée Bantling.

> Désirée had a talent for parties. Sometimes they began presentably and ended outrageously, sometimes they were presentable almost all the time and sometimes they began, continued, and ended outrageously. It was for the last sort that she had gained her notoriety. [12]

One of Lady Bantling's ex-husbands is crushed to death by a massive sewer pipe, and one of the guests, who have all been roving around in the dark looking for clues, must be responsible. Footprints have been obscured, providing an extra challenge for Alleyn.

Death in a White Tie centers around the sociably acceptable "coming-out" party for young ladies during the debutante season. Alleyn's young niece Sarah and her friend Bridget O'Brien become involved in this case. Much of the discussion in the book is taken up with plans for or descriptions of various social functions. The formal ritual of introducing proper young women into polite society for the purpose of finding suitable marriageable males contrasts sharply with the unpleasant business of blackmail engineered by a caterer and a society doctor who abuses his position.

The final play within the play, *The Nursing Home Murder*, is unique: a drama which takes place inside an operating room (also called a "theater"). It encompasses another play within the tale which parallels the murder and misleads the reader.

In the theater of operations Dr. Thoms asks about a new play at the Palladium—a one-act play in which a famous surgeon uses an operation as an opportunity to murder a patient who has ruined him and seduced his wife. Although Thoms says the plot is far-fetched, another doctor and the nurse stare at him. They have both sent threatening letters to the patient on whom they are operating. Jane Harden remarks later that "It is rather like a Greek play.... 'Fate delivers our enemy into our hands.'"[13]

When Sir Derek O'Callaghan dies following a simple appendectomy, the audiences who have seen the play at the Palladium somehow connect the drama with reality, casting Sir John Phillips as the murderer. Nigel, Angela, and Alleyn hear these rumblings when they attend the show out of curiosity. After interviewing him, however, Alleyn declares that if Phillips is guilty, "he's one of the best actors I've ever met."[14]

The final chapter of *The Nursing Home Murder* concludes, like so many of Marsh's tales, with an intensely dramatic dénouement in which the hospital staff—the "theater" party if you will—reenacts the whole operation as precisely as they can while Alleyn and his men observe for opportunities during which murder could be committed.

Alleyn refers to the doctors and nurses as "the star turns."[15] When the "theater party" gathers, they get into the spirit of the performance, carrying out their activities convincingly and doing their best to be about their business at exactly the right moments. A slight accident suddenly upsets them. The murderer is the most nervous member of the cast, hoping that Alleyn will not notice that the anesthesia stand contains a hiding place for the poison with which he killed his patient. Here it may be appropriate to note that P. D. James has used hospital and nursing-home settings and apparatus quite successfully in her works.

In *A Man Lay Dead* the detective convinces the killer to cooperate by demonstrating exactly how he stabbed his victim and got back to his bath in a matter of seconds. While he sets up the reconstruction, Alleyn refers to the "play within the play" and says:

> The buzzer is ringing, the houselights are
> down, the curtain's going up. Take your
> seats, ladies and gentlemen, for the last
> act."16

The religious ritual of *Death in Ecstasy* is dramatic
enough in itself. With his drama critic's eye Nigel suspects
that Jasper Garnett, the priest of the House of the Sacred
Flame, is an actor. His head is that "of an actor, a saint, or
a Middle-West American purveyor of patent medicine."17
After beautiful Cara Quanyne dies dramatically, Nigel
walks up the aisle with "the sensation of walking on to a
stage and joining in the action of the play."18 To get a
better idea of how the murder took place, Alleyn uses his
police team in the place of the cult members and asks them
to pass the sconce from hand to hand. In doing so he tests
out his idea that the darkness would allow poison to be
placed in the cup without anyone's noticing.

In *Death of a Fool* the Sword Wednesday Dance of
the Five Sons reenacts their engagement which allows Alleyn to demonstrate the timing of William Andersen's
bloodless decapitation. Alleyn insists that nothing be left
out of the performance or changed, and that any variations
be reported to him immediately. Suspense builds until Alleyn dramatically leads Mrs. Bünz into the spotlight and
demonstrates how the killer found time to kill the old man
with his bare hands; further he amazes his audience by also
showing how the Fool was murdered.

Once Alleyn knows how an elaborate crime has
been committed he finds it easier to demonstrate rather than
summarize. In this case the murder would seem to be
physically impossible, but once it has been demonstrated by
the participants, everyone can see exactly how it was ac-
complished. Reenactments work better than confusing
explanations.

The reenactment of the final scene of *Macbeth* during which the lead actor is killed in *Light Thickens* comes
just after the murder and does not immediately identify the
killer. This murderer, however, is not sane enough to be
caught in the usual manner. The play itself is more inter-

esting than the murderer, in fact. Alleyn knows *Macbeth* so well that he can ask the actors to begin at

> Blow wind! Come wrack! At least we'll
> die with harness on our back.[19]

He also knows exactly what the necessary technical arrangements are which allows Macbeth to be off stage long enough for the murder to transpire...three minutes.

After the cast has left the scene, Fox and Alleyn reenact the fight (Fox is amazingly agile and catches the spirit of the scene with ease). It takes them four and one-third minutes. Fox picks up a copy of the play, aware that the script is essential to unravelling the mystery of how the murder was committed. The only thing the colleagues overlook is the possibility that someone changed places with another actor. But when things fall together at the end they realize that only one other person could have performed that last scene with such speed and perfect precision.

Another of Marsh's uniquely dramatic devices is her use of properties, articles other than settings and costumes which lend a sense of reality to a stage production. Just as the stage prop is almost part of the cast in a play, the prop in Marsh's novel may be used as weapon, clue, or even motive. Rarely do people simply shoot or poison a victim. often the weapon may be deemed harmless in its everyday use but is employed with deadly effectiveness in a non-conventional manner.

In *Death in a White Tie* Sir Robert Gospell is stunned by a cigarette case and then smothered. Two victims are smashed to death with heavy pottery pigs in *Black as He's Painted*. In *Artists in Crime* an artist's model is posed on an innocuous bench for days in a row, then impaled when a dagger protrudes exactly where it will run through her heart. In *False Scent* Mary Bellamy thoroughly sprays herself with a perfume atomizer filled with a deadly plant spray. *Overture to Death* has a unique booby trap set up inside a piano which causes a pistol to fire with precise aim when the pedal is depressed.   Pigs, perfumes and pianos are ordinarily "safe" objects.

The skewer which rests harmlessly on a hall table in *Death of a Peer* ends up through Lord Wutherwood's eye. In *Vintage Murder* a jeroboam of wine meant for the leading lady's birthday celebration falls devastatingly upon her husband's head when the killer, knowledgeable in stage-craft, changes the scenery weights.   "Wai-a-tapu," a huge pool of boiling mud, becomes an agent of death when the killer in *Colour Scheme* switches white and red flags serving as path markers.

The medicine children are using for ring-worm supplies a murderer with a deadly poison in *Final Curtain*. When they do not lose their hair as they should, the children's teacher is concerned.   But it is not until two people have died, poisoned by *thallium acetate*, the major ingredient in the medicine, that Alleyn learns that the killer emptied part of the bottle's contents and diluted the rest with water.   Thus the victim and his cat, who shared his bedtime milk, are bald.   Here a normal prescription is misused as the agent of a killer.   These everyday objects are harmless enough, until they fall into the wrong, determined hands.

Some weapons which at one time have served as instruments of death seem to be harmless because of their value or antiquity.   These weapons usually are admired by several people in the novel, and thus attract many clear fingerprints before they are put to deadly effect.

The murderer of *Death and the Dancing Footman* uses a *mere*, a beautifully shaped, delicately balanced weapon made of New Zealand greenstone.   In *Black as He's Painted* the first victim is impaled with a ceremonial spear.   In *A Man Lay Dead* a Malay *kriss* emerges as the star in a room full of exotic weapons.   Nearly everyone talks about and handles the beautiful instrument before it turns up in the corpse.

The *claidheamh-mor* (claymore) of *Light Thickens* creates a sense of foreboding in its size and deadliness, and the final battle scene of Macbeth and Macduff is as rigorous and carefully staged as any ballet.   Although the actors know that they are dealing with a dangerous weapon intended to put the enemy to death, no one expects Macbeth to be decapitated during the performance. A similarly deadly slasher, called a *whiffler*, is used to decapitate the Guiser, William Andersen, during the ritual Dance of the Five Sons in *Death of a Fool*.

A few objects serve as red herrings. Two of the novels include Maori *tikis* as props. These fetal figures symbolizing fertility and good luck herald disaster in the context of the novels. Maori actor Rangi Western (in *Light Thickens*) believes that his tiki will protect him against the evils surrounding the production of *Macbeth*. But the primitive appearance of the actor makes him a suspect as well. The tiki appears and vanishes in *Vintage Murder*, and the widow's concern over its disappearance just after her husband's ghastly death surprises those around her. The tiki leads to information about life in New Zealand which has little to do with the murderer's methods or motives.

In several novels clothes cause confusion when they are used as props as well as costumes. Douglas Grace in *Died in the Wool* is knocked unconscious while wearing Alleyn's coat, and Aubrey Mandrake is pushed into the freezing swimming pool wearing another man's Tyrolean cloak in *Death and the Dancing Footman*. The latter episode intentionally casts guilt on the wrong man.

In *Colour Scheme* Geoffrey Gaunt buys a stylish outfit for Barbara hoping to transform the girl whose natural beauty has been obscured by hand-me-downs and her lack of self-confidence. Gaunt's impulse to be a Pygmalion is initially construed as a motive for the murder of Barbara's obnoxious and unwanted suitor. In the same novel, a puce-colored shirt worn by a native of questionable honesty becomes a major clue.

Other objects temporarily throw Alleyn off course. In *A Wreath for Rivera* a good deal is made of a fancy metronome, a jewelled French parasol, and a gun loaded with amateurly prepared blanks. The real weapon is not revealed until late in the novel. A large brass paperweight of a fish *rampant*, a gift from Lady Bantling, nearly kills Pyke Period in *Hand in Glove*, although the sheer silliness of the object parodies an apparently faked pedigree which would have made Mr. Period a logical suspect instead of a possible victim. A book on embalming is used to cast suspicion on Sonia Orrincourt in *Final Curtain*, but the killer's lack of chemical knowledge leads to error when the autopsy uncovers the true cause of death. Without the vindictive action, Sir Henry's death would have continued to be seen as a natural result of serious illness.

Statues of Green Ladies appear with threats of death in *Dead Water*. When Alleyn discovers the body of Elspeth Cost in a pool near Pixie Falls he is afraid that it is Miss Emily Pride, who as owner of the land on which the spurious tourist attraction is located has threatened to put an end to the claims that the spring can effect miracle cures. Although Miss Pride's life had been threatened enough to warrant concern, the victim was the correct one and the assumed motive was totally wrong.

In *When in Rome* another object of value is utilized as a motive for blackmail. Barnaby, a naive young author, loses his briefcase to a street thief. The case contained his manuscript of *Simon in Latium*, which is destined to become a best-seller. Drug dealer Sebastian Mailer convinces Barnaby to use his prestige to attract people with money to Mailer's nightclub (where drugs are readily available), and threatens to accuse him of plagiarizing a simpler manuscript of astonishing similarity to his own. The author is trapped until Alleyn frees him of all charges, including the murder.

In *Clutch of Constables* Hazel Rickerby-Carrick's Fabergé "zodiac" pin is a family heirloom so tempting that the professional art fraud ring on board ship with her cannot resist keeping it when she has to be silenced for other reasons. Up to that point, although Alleyn was pursuing the notorious "Jampot" ring, he had no idea that his wife would be the one to spot the false Constable painting and notice that Hazel had not merely left the ship early. Poor Hazel had also stumbled upon the link between the people on the boat and had recorded the information in her journal. The journal—not the heirloom—was the motive for her murder.

The Shakespearean relic, Hamnet's glove (belonging to Shakespeare's son), is priceless in itself and also as a publicity gimmick in *Killer Dolphin*. It inspires Peregrine Jay's play and causes old enmities to surface. One talented man risks his career in making a copy of it to prevent a national treasure from being sent to America. The value of the object could drive anyone to murder, but the "murder" that does occur is an accident.

The death which results from a quest to own the valuable Black Alexander stamp is *not* accidental. The stamp is hidden on Captain Carter's estate in *Grave Mistake*, and the Captain, who was killed in World War I, left no instructions to assist his wife in finding the legacy. In *Night at the Vulcan* blackmail is objectified in the form of a letter with a foreign stamp which catches the eye of Clark Bennington, and informs him that Dr. John Rutherford has merely translated a brilliant play by one of his wife's own lovers in order to pass it off as his own. Bennington's gleeful knowledge, however, gets him killed. Marsh's motives for murder are usually linked to character rather than possessions. The Black Alexander and the foreign letter are exceptions to her rule.

Usually the props Marsh introduces into her works are used as clues rather than weapons or motives. The earlier novels are filled with ordinary items which disappear and reappear in time to assist Alleyn in identifying a killer. Gloves are featured in *Killer Dolphin, Hand in Glove, A Man Lay Dead*, and *Enter a Murderer*, while cigarette cases help catch the murderer in *Death in a White Tie, Hand in Glove* (again), and *Died in the Wool*.

Try as he may, Sam Whipplestone cannot ignore the pottery fish pendant Lucy Lockett carries off from his tenants. The pendant is a clue for Alleyn, enabling him to identify a secret anti-Ng'ombwanan group in *Black as He's Painted*. The little silver goat Ricky Alleyn carries about with him in *Spinsters in Jeopardy* helps his parents locate him when he is abducted, and also points to the devil worshipping drug cult for which Alleyn has been searching. Too much glass on the floor bothers Alleyn in *Death at the Bar* until he discovers that there were *two* bottles of disinfectant, one innocent and one which held the poison. A bottle and two glasses take on significance when Fox is poisoned by some extremely fine wine.

Some killers leave hints in the form of objects which later serve as clues. The psychopathic killer of *Singing in the Shrouds* leaves behind flowers, a broken necklace, and a song. In *Photo Finish* Alleyn discovers an Italian book about the murder of Bianca Rossi—which explains why opera singer Isabella Sommita must die. Other props, including an unflattering photo of La Sommita, wrongly suggest that Strix, the photographer, is involved, until Alleyn realizes that Italian revenge is at the root of his case. In *The Nursing Home Murder* the murderer notches his stethescope every time he destroys an "unfit specimen."

Some killers try to hide their crimes to the best of their abilities, only to have their schemes spoiled by animals. Pixie, Harold Cartell's effervescently disobedient dog, crashes into a room with the glove which traps the killer in *Hand in Glove*. A cat, Mrs. Thomasina Twitchett, does not eat all the fish that Kitty Carterette tries to feed her, and the remains discovered by a perceptive constable provide the proof needed to conclude the mystery. Since no two fish have the same scale patterns (something like fingerprints) the scales clinging to Kitty's golf skirt give her away, thus explaining the title of *Scales of Justice*! A medallion found by an abused kitten in *Black as He's Painted* helps Alleyn uncover the plot and explains who murdered two people with pottery pigs. Mungo the dangerous horse of *Last Ditch* is a significant part of the plot.

Each novel has unique props appropriate to the world of the book and as diverse as the dart board of *Death at the Bar*. The trappings of witchcraft create colorful moments in *Death of a Peer*, especially when juxtaposed against numerous references to *Macbeth*. Witchcraft and goodluck charms abound in *Light Thickens*.

Marsh's worlds in fact are filled with vivid objects as well as unique and interesting people, and all are introduced much as a prop man would do for a drama company. Each is appropriate to its milieu, and each serves a purpose. These colorful objects have the charm and appeal of the props and settings utilized in *Clue*, the popular mystery game based on the British country house murder plot. Whether it is an object to set the scene, a device to mislead those searching for a murderer, a desirable item which becomes a motive for the murder itself, a genuine clue, a series of "red herrings," or the murder weapon itself, Marsh has the ability to establish an illusion of reality through concrete objects.

Whether she is portraying life backstage or on a New Zealand sheep ranch, Marsh's audience can visualize the entire setting. When Marsh began writing fiction, with *A Man Lay Dead.* she used the familiar drawing room setting of a society house party. Following that somewhat clichéd backdrop, however, she began to incorporate her beloved theater into her detective stories, and brought to them a reality and polish they might have lacked if she had remained with a more conventional approach. Her detailed use of her background and experience as part of a theatrical company made her mysteries special and brought her continuing success.

VI.

FINAL ACT

NGAIO MARSH AND HER DETECTIVE FICTION

Ngaio Marsh is without doubt an enduring and talented writer of mysteries. Inspector Alleyn, his wife Troy, and his partner Teddy Fox are assured a permanent place among the literary crime solvers of all time, along with Sherlock Holmes and Dr. Watson, *et al.* Marsh's talent, however, is limited when compared to genre writers like Ross Macdonald and P. D. James, who are especially skilled at psychological characterization. Marsh has chosen to limit her writing to the clichés of the theater and the conventions of traditional British "genteel" mystery novels. She rarely goes beyond superficial maneuverings of plot and character, and seldom reaches any great depth in her narrative and characterizations. The very elements which have made her work of interest to and popular with her fans have also made them transitory and less satisfactory for deeper study.

While Marsh has created a distinctive and consistent hero in Alleyn, she has not quite succeeded in turning him into a "real" human being. Alleyn is the theatrical "star," seen on a stage against an artificial backdrop. His costars, Troy and Fox, are interesting, but their second billing does not allow the reader to see them as fully-realized personas. Troy *does* play an important part, particularly in a work like *Clutch of Constables*, where she remains center stage for a good portion of the book. But as soon as the murder is committed and it becomes clear that the notorious "Jampot" is involved in the crime, the resourceful, independent woman goes mildly away while her husband finishes the important business of solving the crime.

Marsh's use of Shakespearean conventions of drama are her most memorable qualities, and provide her faithful readers who share her love for the stage, with a great deal of reciprocal pleasure. Identifying allusions and parallels is a delightful game—almost as enjoyable as solving the crime before the final chapter. But these literary references provide no real insights into human nature, and unlike her mentor, Shakespeare, Marsh today is generally not quoted.

The greatest identifiable weakness in Marsh's prose remains her exposition of motive, which inevitably is presented from Alleyn's point of view that the *opportunity* for committing the crime is more significant than the *reason* for committing the crime. Marsh's characters tend to kill others for the convenience of her plot, or simply because a weapon has come to hand. They seem nearly as driven as Macbeth to do deeds that in themselves seem to be fated by the gods.

While Alleyn seems to have sympathy for his killers, he will never mourn them. Alleyn seems like a cool "mechanic." He does and says all the right things, but he is no tortured soul like Lew Archer (Ross Macdonald's P.I.) or suffering artist like Adam Dalgliesh (P. D. James' creation). While Archer and Dalgleish go beyond logic to empathy, Alleyn can never see himself as a potential criminal. He can never get into the mind or under the skin of his killers—he can only track their logical steps.

The reason for this lack of empathy seem to be that Alleyn has never suffered. He has not experienced divorce and loneliness, nor has he faced the death of a beloved wife or child. He is a detective without pain. He *is* vulnerable to romantic interludes; in *Enter a Murderer* Stephanie Vaughan nearly "steals his heart" (as he puts it), and Troy must play hard-to-get, forcing him to work hard to win her. But even in his love life Alleyn seems to be blessed. Since he has never known great sorrow, it is difficult, if not impossible, for him to understand how people might be driven to commit violent and despicable acts.

In summary, Marsh is a competent technician, but not a brilliant one; she is an amiable story-teller—but not an outstanding one. Some of her book cover blurbs refer to

her as "better than Christie," but while her style and characterization may be significant, she cannot compete with
Christie's overall ability to create memorable plots. Marsh
has little or no insight into the sordidness and pain which
infects human lives—nor does she have the power to convey such evil in the same spellbinding manner as Christie.

Ngaio Marsh gave every appearance of having lived
a contented, fulfilled life. Her autobiography, *Black Beech
and Honeydew* fairly pulses with wonder at the beauty of
her world. "O Brave New World" could well have been
her characteristic utterance; certainly her protagonist Alleyn
conveys that sense of wonder, in spite of his upper class
sophistication. Author and hero alike inspire loyalty and
affection among their cohorts—and both go "by the book"
in terms of their conventionality.

Ngaio Marsh began her first book, *A Man Lay
Dead*, as a lark. She never took her work as a detective
fiction writer as seriously as she did her great contributions
to the arts, and it would be a mistake for us to do so. For
Marsh, bringing her beloved Shakespeare's works to the
people of her country was her first priority. Although she
did not achieve wide literary acclaim as did such writers as
Ross Macdonald and P. D. James, she still has earned a
well-deserved place in the ranks of the great artists of the
fictional crime, along with Dorothy Sayers, Margery
Allingham and Agatha Christie. Our greatest tribute to her
is in the continued enjoyment of her work.

APPENDIX III
SHAKESPEARE'S CHARACTERS IN MARSH'S WORKS

CHARACTER	TITLE	PLAY
Geoffrey Gaunt	*Colour Scheme*	*Henry IV*
Martyn Tarne "Kate"	*Night at the Vulcan*	*Taming of the Shrew*
Mr. Oberon	*Spinsters in Jeopardy*	*Midsummer Night's Dream*
Robin Grey	*Death of a Peer*	*Midsummer Night's Dream*
Helena Hamilton	*Night at Vulcan*	*Midsummer... & All's Well...*
Robin Jay	*Light Thickens*	*Henry V & Richard III*
Robin Herrington	*Spinsters in Jeopardy*	*Henry V & Richard III*
George Alleyn	*Black...He's Painted*	*Henry VI*
Richard Jay	*Light Thickens*	*Henry VI, Richard II & III*
Richard Dakers	*False Scent*	*Henry VI, Richard II & III*
Simon Morten	*Light Thickens*	*Richard II*
Stephanie Vaughan	*Enter a Murderer*	*Richard III*
Nurse/Nanny	*False Scent*	*Romeo and Juliet*
Mr. Mortimer	*Final Curtain*	*Henry IV & Henry VI*
Margaret Mannering	*Light Thickens*	*Henry VI*
Edward Max	*Wreath for Rivera*	*Henry VI*
Douglas Grace	*Died in the Wool*	*Henry IV*
Julia Pharamond	*Last Ditch*	*Romeo and Juliet*
Robin Grey/Jay	*Death of a Peer*	*Merry Wives of Windsor*
Robin Grey/Jay	*Light Thickens*	*Merry Wives of Windsor*
Bruce Gardener	*Grave Mistake*	*Richard II*
Felix Gardener	*Enter a Murderer*	*Richard II*
Carlisle Wayne	*A Wreath for Rivera*	*Richard II*
Richard (Ricky)	*Spinsters in Jeopardy*	*Richard II, Richard III*
Richard (Ricky)	*Last Ditch*	*Henry VI*
Adam Poole	*Night at the Vulcan*	*All's Well that Ends Well*
Maria, the maid	*Photo Finish*	*Twelfth Night*
Fabian Losse	*Died in the Wool*	*Twelfth Night*
Jacques Dore	*Night at the Vulcan*	*All's Well that Ends Well*
Lord Baggott	*A Wreath for Rivera*	*Richard II*
Crispin Jay	*Light Thickens*	*Henry V*
Octavius Brown	*False Scent*	*Julius Caesar*
Marcus Knight	*Night at the Vulcan*	*Julius Caesar*
Octavius	*Scales of Justice*	*Julius Caesar*
Richard Oates	*Death at the Bar*	*Richard II*
Isabella Sommita	*Photo Finish*	*Measure For Measure*
Emily Jay (Emilia)	*Killer Dolphin*	*Othello*
Emily Jay (Emilia)	*Light Thickens*	*Othello*
Cressida Tottenham	*Tied Up in Tinsel*	*Troilus and Cressida*
Bianca Rossi	*Photo Finish*	*Taming of the Shrew*
Desdemona	*Final Curtain*	*Othello*
"Desdemona"	*Death of a Fool*	*Othello*
Troy Alleyn	*Scales of Justice*	*Troilus and Cressida*
John Rutherford	*Night at the Vulcan*	*King John*
William	*Killer Dolphin*	*The Sonnets*
Destiny Mead	*Killer Dolphin*	*The Sonnets*
Gertrude Bracey	*Killer Dolphin*	*Hamlet*
Paul & Paula Kentish	*Final Curtain*	*King Lear*
Montague Reece	*Photo Finish*	*Romeo and Juliet*
Montague Marchant	*False Scent*	*Romeo and Juliet*
Timon Gantry	*False Scent*	*Timon of Athens*
Violetta (Viola)	*When in Rome*	*Twelfth Night*

NOTES

CHAPTER ONE

1Ngaio Marsh, *Black Beech and Honeydew*. Boston: Little, Brown, 1965, p. 302.
2She reports that he made at least two exciting arrests, one of "a famous sheep-stealer," and another "a gigantic Negro murderer," *ibid.*, p. 24.
3A similar relic, associated directly with Shakespeare, is the basis for the plot of *Killer Dolphin*.
4She discusses her writing procedure in *The Great Detectives*, ed. Otto Penzler. Boston: Little, Brown, 1978, p. 258.
5 Dr. Jellett had helped her through a three month hospitalization during which she had had a series of minor operations and one "final snorter of a major one," *ibid.*, p. 264.
6Earl F. Bargainnier has written an exemplary critical work on Marsh. See: "Ngaio Marsh," in *10 Women of Mystery*, ed. Earl F. Bargainnier. Bowling Green: Popular Press, 1981, p. 78-105.
7In Earl F. Bargainnier, "Ngaio Marsh's 'Theatrical' Murders," in *Armchair Detective* (1977).
8LeRoy Panek, in *Watteau's Shepherds: The Detective Story in Britain, 1914-1940*, Bowling Green: Popular Press, 1979, ch. 9.
9*Ibid.*

CHAPTER TWO

1*Night at the Vulcan*. Boston: Little, Brown, 1951, p. 272.
2*Killer Dolphin*. Garden City, NY: Doubleday, 1966, p. 436.
3*A Man Lay Dead*. New York: Jove, 1978, p. 163.
4*Ibid.*, p. 41.
5*Ibid.*, p. 45.
6*Ibid.*, p. 113.
7*Ibid.*, p. 140.
8*Ibid.*
9*Ibid.*, p. 170.
10*Enter a Murderer*. New York: Berkley Medallion, 1977, p. 20.
11*Ibid.*, p. 21.
12*Ibid.*, p. 63.
13*Ibid.*, p. 179.
14*Ibid.*, p. 249.

15*A Man Lay Dead*, p. 144.
16*When in Rome*. New York: Berkley Medallion, 1978, p. 49.
17*Colour Scheme·* New York: Jove, 1982, p. 113.
18*Ibid.*, p. 152.
19*Spinsters in Jeopardy*. In *Grave Mistake, and Two Other Great Mysteries*. Boston: Little, Brown, 1953, p. 238.
20*A Man Lay Dead*, p. 68.
21*Enter a Murderer*, p. 79.
22*Ibid.*, p. 80.
23*Ibid.*, p. 82.
24*False Scent*. New York: Jove, 1978, p. 112.
25*A Wreath for Rivera*. In *Photo Finish and Two Other Great Mysteries*. Garden City, NY: Doubleday, 1980, p. 230.
26*Death of a Peer*. New York: Jove, 1980, p. 136.
27*Light Thickens*. Boston: Little, Brown, 1982, p. 115.
28*Night at the Vulcan*, p. 299.
29*False Scent*, p. 80.
30*Death in a White Tie*. New York: Jove, 1980, p. 108.
31*Ibid.*, p. 179.
32*Tied Up in Tinsel*. New York: Jove, 1978, p. 254.
33*Scales of Justice*. Boston: Little, Brown, 1955, p. 133.
34*Vintage Murder*. New York: Jove, 1978, p. 197.
35*Death at the Bar*. New York: Jove, 1980, p. 225.
36*Ibid.*, p. 228.
37*Hand in Glove*. New York: Jove, 1980, p. 183.
38*Scales of Justice*, p. 262.
39*Death at the Bar*, p. 218.
40*Grave Mistake*, p. 117-118.
41*Ibid.*, p. 122.
42*Wreath for Rivera*, p. 330
43*Final Curtain*. New York: Jove, 1980, p. 110.
44*Ibid.*, p. 19.
45*Clutch of Constables*. New York: Berkley Medallion, 1978, p. 107.
46*Photo Finish*, p. 153.

CHAPTER THREE

1*Enter a Murderer*, p. 22.
2*Ibid.*, p. 23.
3*Ibid.*, p. 25.
4*Ibid.*, p. 28.
5*Ibid.*, p. 45.
6*Ibid.*, p. 62.
7*Ibid.*, p. 12.
8*Ibid.*, p. 65.
9*Ibid.*, p. 97.

[10]*Ibid.*, p. 163.
[11]*Ibid.*, p. 179.
[12]*Ibid.*, p. 235.
[13]*Ibid.*, p. 149.
[14]*False Scent*, p. 8.
[15]*Ibid.*, p. 81.
[16]*Final Curtain*, p. 6.
[17]*Ibid.*, p. 11.
[18]*Ibid.*, p. 60-61.
[19]*Ibid.*
[20]*Ibid.*
[21]*Ibid.*
[22]*Photo Finish*, p. 7.
[23]*Ibid.*
[24]*Light Thickens*, p. 45.
[25]*Ibid.*, p. 37.
[26]*Ibid.*, p. 5.
[27]*Ibid.*, p. 8.
[28]*Ibid.*, p. 171.
[29]*Vintage Murder*, p. 268.
[30]*Ibid.*, p. 17.
[31]*Ibid.*, p. 17-18.
[32]*Ibid.*, p. 83.
[33]*Ibid.*, p. 38-39.
[34]*Ibid.*, p. 49.
[35]*Killer Dolphin*, p. 434.
[36]*Ibid.*, p. 392.
[37]*Ibid.*, p. 422.
[38]*Ibid.*, p. 393.
[39]*Ibid.*, p. 402.
[40]*Ibid.*, p. 403.
[41]*Ibid.*, p. 413.
[42]*Ibid.*, p. 423.
[43]*Ibid.*, p. 414.
[44]*Night at the Vulcan*, p. 173.
[45]*Ibid.*, p. 189.
[46]*Ibid.*, p. 193.
[47]*Ibid.*, p. 230-231.
[48]*Ibid.*, p. 273.
[49]*Ibid.*, p. 295.
[50]*Ibid.*, p. 307.
[51]*Ibid.*, p. 308.
[52]*Ibid.*, p. 207.
[53]*Singing in the Shrouds*, p. 56.
[54]*Spinsters in Jeopardy*, p. 264.
[55]*Ibid.*, p. 287.

56*Ibid.*, p. 289.
57*Ibid.*, p. 291.
58*Overture to Death.* In *Grave Mistake...*, *ibid.*, p. 449.
59*Ibid.*, p. 481.
60*Ibid.*, p. 447.
61*A Wreath for Rivera*, p. 221.
62*Ibid.*, p. 220.
63*Death of a Fool.* New York: Jove, 1978, p. 29.
64*Ibid.*, p. 39.
65*Ibid.*, p. 140.
66*Ibid.*, p. 142.
67*Ibid.*, p. 143.
68*Ibid.*, p. 152.
69*Ibid.*, p. 199.
70*Ibid.*, p. 218.
71*Ibid.*, p. 228.
72*Grave Mistake*, p. 67.
73*Ibid.*, p. 137.
74*Ibid.*, p. 146.
75*Ibid.*, p. 212.
76*Ibid.*, p. 24.
77*Death in a White Tie*, p. 155.
78*Ibid.*, p. 159.
79*Ibid.*
80*Ibid.*, p. 163.
81*Tied Up in Tinsel*, p. 32.
82*Ibid.*, p. 89-90.
83*Death at the Bar*, p. 18.
84*Ibid.*, p. 110.
85*Ibid.*, p. 130.
86*Ibid.*, p. 135-136.
87*Killer Dolphin*, p. 460.
88*A Wreath for Rivera*, p. 373.

CHAPTER FOUR

1*Night at the Vulcan*, p. 321.
2*Spinters in Jeopardy*, p. 227.
3*Ibid.*, p. 234.
4*Ibid.*, p. 344.
5*The Nursing Home Murder*, p. 235.
6*Spinsters in Jeopardy*, p. 326-327.
7*Night at the Vulcan*, p. 315.
8*Ibid.*, p. 316.
9*Ibid.*, p. 233.
10*Ibid.*, p. 234.

11*Black as He's Painted.* Boston: Little, Brown, 1973, p. 116.
12*Ibid.*, p. 222.
13*Singing in the Shrouds*, p. 18.
14*Ibid.*, p. 138.
15*Ibid.*, p. 140.
16*Ibid.*, p. 179.
17*Ibid.*, p. 181.
18*Ibid.*, p. 234.
19*Scales of Justice*, p. 63.
20*Hand in Glove*, p. 130.
21*Ibid.*, p. 162.
22*Last Ditch.* New York: Berkley Medallion, 1978, p. 171.
23*Ibid.*, p. 174.
24*Death of a Fool*, p. 43.
25*Ibid.*
26*Ibid.*, p. 126.
27*Ibid.*, p. 118.
28*Ibid.*, p. 132.
29*Ibid.*, p. 134.
30*Ibid.*, p. 198.
31*Ibid.*, p. 243.
32*Ibid.*, p. 252.
33*Death of a Peer*, p. 105, 233.
34*Ibid.*, p. 42-43.
35*Ibid.*, p. 163.
36*Ibid.*, p. 164.
37*Ibid.*, p. 272.
38*Ibid.*, p. 194, 302.
39*Ibid.*, p. 230.
40*Ibid.*
41*Ibid.*, p. 242.
42*Ibid.*, p. 243.
43*Ibid.*, p. 295.
44*Ibid.*, p. 296.
45*Scales of Justice*, p. 160.
46II, p. 1667-1670.
47*Enter a Murderer*, p. 188.
48*Died in the Wool.* New York: Berkley Medallion, 1978, p. 57.
49*Death in a White Tie*, p. 287.
50*Death of a Peer*, p. 43.
51*Overture to Death.* In *Grave Mistake...*, p. 481.
52*Death and the Dancing Footman.* New York: Jove, 1980, p. 201.
53*Dead Water.* New York: Berkley, 1961, p. 63.
54*Death at the Bar*, p. 184.
55*Clutch of Constables*, p. 157.
56*A Wreath for Rivera*, p. 231.

57*Dead Water*, p. 141.
58*Ibid.*, p. 271.
59*Final Curtain*, p. 90.
60*Ibid.*, p. 91.
61*Ibid.*, p. 94.
62*Ibid.*, p. 186.
63*Light Thickens*, p. 135.
64*A Man Lay Dead*, p. 167.
65*Tied Up in Tinsel*, p. 237-238.

CHAPTER FIVE

1*The Nursing Home Murders*, p. 174.
2*Ibid.*, p. 177-178.
3*Death in Ecstasy*. New York: Jove, 1980, p. 134-135.
4*Enter a Murderer*, p. 39.
5*Death and the Dancing Footman*, p. 14.
6*Ibid.*, p. 294.
7*Singing in the Shrouds*, p. 103.
8*Ibid.*, p. 104.
9*Ibid.*, p. 79.
10*Ibid.*, p. 107.
11*Dead Water*, p. 100.
12*Hand in Glove*, p. 89.
13*The Nursing Home Murders*, p. 35.
14*Ibid.*, p. 194.
15*Ibid.*, p. 208.
16*A Man Lay Dead*, p. 179.
17*Death in Ecstasy*, p. 8.
18*Ibid.*, p. 14.
19*Light Thickens*, p. 127.

SELECTED PRIMARY BIBLIOGRAPHY

Artists in Crime. New York: Jove, 1980 (1938).

Black as He's Painted. London: Collins; Boston: Little, Brown, 1974.

Black Beech and Honeydew. Boston: Little, Brown, 1965.

Clutch of Constables. New York: Berkley Medallion, 1978 (c1968).

Colour Scheme. New York. Jove, 1982 (1943).

Dead Water. New York: Berkley, 1961.

Death and the Dancing Footman. New York: Jove, 1980 (c1941).

Death at the Bar. New York: Jove, 1980 (c1940).

Death in Ecstasy. New York: Jove, 1980 (c1936).

Death in a White Tie. New York: Jove, 1980 (c1938).

Death of a Fool. New York: Jove, 1978 (c1956).

Death of a Peer. New York: Jove, 1980 (c1940).

Died in the Wool. New York: Berkley Medallion, 1978 (c1945).

Enter a Murderer. New York: Berkley Medallion, 1977 (c1935).

False Scent. New York: Jove, 1978 (c1960).

Final Curtain. New York: Jove, 1980 (c1947).

Grave Mistake. In collection, *Grave Mistake and Two Others* (rpt. Boston: Little, Brown, 1978).

Hand in Glove. New York: Jove, 1980 (c1962).

Killer Dolphin. Boston: Little, Brown, 1966.

Last Ditch. New York: Berkley Medallion, 1978 (c1977).

Light Thickens. London: Collins; Boston: Little, Brown, 1982.

A Man Lay Dead. New York: Jove, 1978 (c1934).

New Zealand (for children). New York: Macmillan, 1964.

Night at the Vulcan. Boston: Little, Brown, 1951 (rpt. of *Opening Night.* London: Collins, 1951).

The Nursing Home Murder, with Henry Jellett.   Boston: Little, Brown, 1972 (c1935).

Overture to Death.   In collection, *Grave Mistake and Two Others* (rpt. London: Collins; New York: Furman, 1939.

Photo-Finish.   In *Photo-Finish and Two Other Great Mysteries*.   Garden City, New York: Doubleday, 1980 (rpt. London: Collins; Boston: Little, Brown, 1980).

Scales of Justice.   London: Collins; Boston: Little, Brown, 1955.

Singing in the Shrouds.   New York: Jove, 1978 (c1958).

Spinsters in Jeopardy.   In collection *Grave Mistake and Two Others* (rpt. Boston: Little, Brown, 1953).

Tied Up in Tinsel.   New York: Jove, 1978 (c1972).

Vintage Murder.   New York: Jove, 1978 (c1937).

When in Rome.   New York: Berkley Medallion, 1978 (c1971).

A Wreath for Rivera.   In *Photo Finish...* (1949).

SELECTED SECONDARY BIBLIOGRAPHY

Bargainnier, Earl F. "Ngaio Marsh," in *10 Women of Mystery*, ed. Earl F. Bargainnier. Bowling Green: Popular Press, 1981, p. 78-105.

Bargainnier, Earl F. "Ngaio Marsh's 'Theatrical' Murders," in *Armchair Detective* 10 (1977): 175-181.

Bargainnier, Earl F. "Roderick Alleyn: Ngaio Marsh's Oxonian Superintendent," in *Armchair Detective* 11 (1978): 63-71.

Frye, Roland Mushat. *Shakespeare—The Art of the Dramatist*. Boston: Houghton Mifflin Co., 1970.

Grella, George. "Murder and Manners: The Formal Detective Novel," in *Novel* 4 (Fall, 1970): 30-48.

Gwilt, Peter R. and John R. Gwilt. "The Use of Poison in Detective Fiction," in *Clues* 1 (Fall/Winter, 1980): 8-17.

Haycroft, Howard. *Murder for Pleasure: The Life and Times of The Detective Story*, enlarged ed. New York: Biblo and Tannen, 1968.

Hipolito, Jane. "Reviews of *When in Rome* and *Tied Up in Tinsel*," in *Mystery and Detective Annual* (1972): 233-236.

Hoffman, Nancy Y. "Mistresses of Malfeasance," in *Dimensions of Detective Fiction*, edited by Larry N. Landrum, Ray B. Browne, and Pat Browne. Bowling Green: Bowling Green State University Popular Press, 1976, p. 97-101.

Lachman, Marvin. "It's About Crime," in *The Mystery Fancier* 6 (Nov.-Dec., 1982): 19-20.

Mann, Jessica. "Ngaio Marsh," in *Deadlier than the Male*. New York: Macmillan, 1981, p. 218-233.

Marsh, Ngaio. "Entertainments," in *Pacific Quarterly* 3 (Jan., 1978): 27-32.

Marsh, Ngaio. "Portrait of Troy," in *Murderess Ink*, edited by Dilys Winn. New York: Workman Publishing, 1979, p. 142-144.

Marsh, Ngaio. "Roderick Alleyn," in *The Great Detectives*, edited by Otto Penzler. Boston: Little, Brown, 1978, p. 2-8.

"Milestones." *Time* 119 (1 March 1982): 89 (obituary of "Ngaio Marsh, 82").

Panek, LeRoy. *Watteau's Shepherd's: The Detective Novel in Britain, 1914-1940*. Bowling Green: Bowling Green State University Popular Press, 1979, p. 185-197.

Slung, Michelle. "Women in Detective Fiction," in *The Mystery Story*, edited by John Ball. Baltimore: Penguin Books, 1976, p. 125-140.

Symons, Julian. *Mortal Consequences*. New York: Schocken Books, 1973.

INDEX

CHARACTERS

143

www.ingramcontent.com/pod-product-compliance
Lightning Source LLC
Chambersburg PA
CBHW021236090426
42740CB00006B/559